I0394471

THE CREATION TAPESTRY
OF GIRONA (SPAIN) FROM AROUND 1100

When Paganism, Judaism,
Christianity and Islam were United

by
Hansueli F. Etter

CHIRON PUBLICATIONS • ASHEVILLE, NORTH CAROLINA

© 2020 by Chiron Publications. All rights reserved. No part of this publication may be reproduced, stored in a retrieval system, or transmitted, in any form by any means, electronic, mechanical, photocopying, recording, or otherwise, without the prior written permission of the publisher, Chiron Publications, P.O. Box 19690, Asheville, N.C. 28815-1690.

www.ChironPublications.com

Cover design by Martina Ott
Interior design by Danijela Mijailovic
Printed primarily in the United States of America.

ISBN 978-1-63051-784-7 paperback
ISBN 978-1-63051-785-4 hardcover
ISBN 978-1-63051-786-1 electronic
ISBN 978-1-63051-787-8 limited edition paperback

Library of Congress Cataloging-in-Publication Data

Names: Etter, Hansueli F., author. | Etter, Hansueli F. Schöpfungsteppich von Girona.

Title: The Creation tapestry of Girona (Spain) from around 1100 : when paganism, Judaism, Christianity and Islam were united / by Hansueli F. Etter.

Other titles: Schöpfungsteppich von Girona. English

Description: Asheville, North Carolina : Chiron Publications, [2020] | Includes bibliographical references. | Summary: "Around the year 1100 a genius mind created an image which has not lost its meaning today-the Creation Tapestry. To discover the symbolic meaning of the rich iconography of the Creation Tapestry opens up an insight in the common background of all religions back to the roots of shamanism, which use mandalas in dance as well as in images"—Provided by publisher.

Identifiers: LCCN 2020049025 (print) | LCCN 2020049026 (ebook) | ISBN 9781630517847 (paperback) | ISBN 9781630517854 (hardcover) | ISBN 9781630517861 (ebook)

Subjects: LCSH: Tapís de la creació. | Christian art and symbolism—Spain—Gerona—Medieval, 500-1500. | Mandala. | Tapestry, Romanesque—Spain—Gerona. | Catedral de Girona.

Classification: LCC NK3062.G47 E8813 2020 (print) | LCC NK3062.G47 (ebook) | DDC 704.9/482—dc23

LC record available at https://lccn.loc.gov/2020049025

LC ebook record available at https://lccn.loc.gov/2020049026

Table of Contents

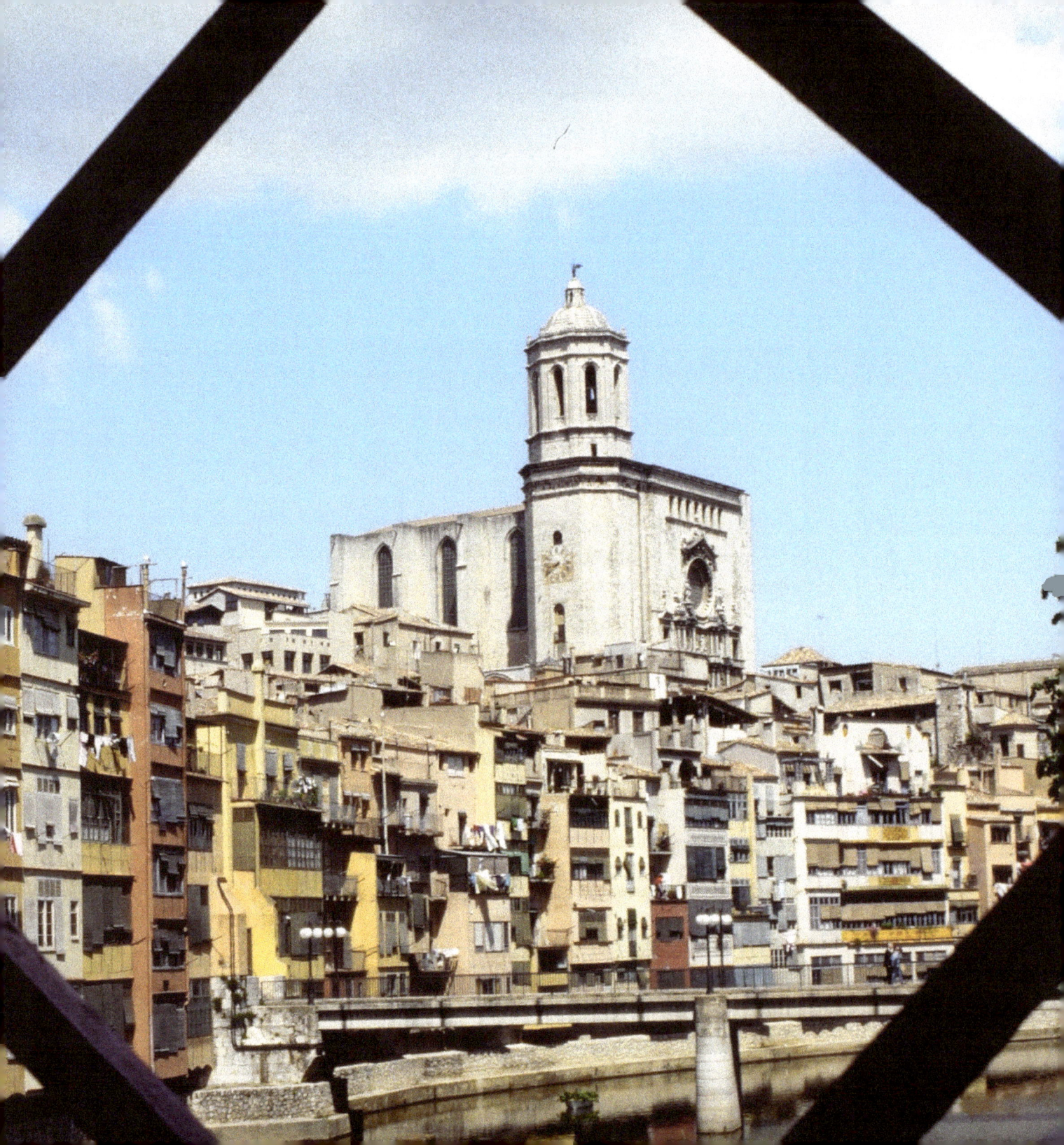

Personal Foreword

In 1982 I visited the Cathedral of Gerona in Catalonia (Spain) as a tourist. There I met the Creation Tapestry for the first time. It was meant to be a fateful encounter. A year later in February 1983, the Bishop of Gerona Jaume Camprodon (1926-2016) allowed me to examine the Creation Tapestry in the Museum of the Cathedral, which was closed to the public during these cold winter days. During an audience, he gave me insights into his own relationship to this outstanding work of art. The archaeologist Dr. Jürg Schneider (Zurich), and the photographer and excavation technician Jürg Hanser (Zurich) – I worked closely with them at the time – have accompanied me. From both colleagues I received many professional hints.

Back in Switzerland, the documents of my investigation as well as the photographic documentation of this art object were available to me. The yearly visits added a lot of experiences and insights. I hoped to find an answer to the questions, why the Creation Tapestry is fascinating me and 10,000s of annual visitors, why this medieval image still enthralls today an amount of interests that goes far beyond an art-historical curiosity. After extensive studies I dared to reconstruct the missing parts at the bottom of the picture, since the basic concept is undoubtedly a mandala. The added images should fit sensibly into the essential statement of the Creation Tapestry. Finally, my lasting fascination gave me the necessary energy to add to the many art-historical publications a new one, which wanted to open up a different view of the Creation Tapestry.

I received particularly valuable suggestions on the symbolic content of the tapestry and its cross-cultural allusions again and again from Dr. Marie-Louise von Franz, Küsnacht (1915-1998). I was also in contact with Pedro de Palol (1923-2005), professor of medieval archaeology at the University of Barcelona, who had published several fundamental art-historical discussions on the tapestry. On the occasion of a visit, his reaction to my question about the Arab influence on the tapestry sparked me off to ponder more over it. I like to remember the numerous questions and hints from readers, as well as participants on the occasion of the many lectures and trips to the tapestry, which encouraged me to deepen my work.

The first opportunity to publish my work in German came in 1989 through the Foundation for Jungian Psychology, Küsnacht, which had launched a new series of publications at the time. I am very grateful to Alison Kappes, Hirzel, who took the initiative and the effort to translate thereafter my manuscript into English and to Anita Zäh, Zürich, who added recently the English footnotes and updated the bibliography. To my delight, Jungian Psychologist Dukkyu Kim (Seoul) published the book in 2019 in a particularly beautiful edition in Korean. From the friendly contact with Len Cruz and Steve Buser of Chiron Publication (Asheville, North Carolina) developed the idea of adding an edition in English. With Jennifer Fitzgerald, editor and general manager at Chiron Publication, I had an empathetic, patient, competent and determined person at my disposal. Martina Ott, graphic designer in Zurich, helped to design the book cover.

I am very grateful to all these people, because they helped the Creation Tapestry and its content to become known as new. But most grateful, I am to all the unknown creators of the Creation Tapestry, who left us with their creative, intellectual and craftsmanship activities a medieval masterpiece from around 1100, the symbolic significance of which has lost nothing till the present days. I hope the Creation Tapestry will find its way into the modern human psyche and will create its healing effect as well.

Küsnacht, 24th April 2020
Hansueli Etter

Preface

Around the year 1100 a genius mind—woman or man—created an image, which has not lost its meaning till today. It was made by hundreds of busy hands as a colorful gobelin most probably used originally for centuries as a canopy in the Romanesque Cathedral of Gerona, North east of Spain. The original tapestry showed all signs of a mandala: a big circle surrounded by a square with a central symbol and many interesting details. What makes this mandala unique, is the fact that it unites pagan symbols in the form of nature gods (rivers, winds, the year), of the genesis of the Jewish Tora (the creation myth), of the holy cross of Christianity hold by the roman emperor Constantine the Great and according to Muslim tradition of the tapestry as a whole and its mandala shape. Nowadays a part at the bottom of the tapestry is missing, but the still visible iconographic details and the understanding of its meaning allowed a full reconstruction of the image.

During the late medieval time a Muslim bath was built in Gerona close to the dominating Romanesque Cathedral and not far from the Jewish synagogue, all together well protected within the walls of the town. Pagan, Jewish, Christian and Muslim cultures and traditions were well flourishing and were inspiring each other without prejudices. It was perhaps the last ecumenical coexistence of different religions, which ended around 1500, when the last Moorish Caliph of Granada was forced to desert Spain and all the Spanish Jews had to leave Spain. At the same time Christopher Colombo sailed to the west under the protection of the *Virgin Mary on the pillar* and brought illness, devastation and even extinction to the indigenous people. Spain turned into a gigantic powerful and intolerant country under the reign of the catholic Queen Isabelle and King Ferdinand. *The Tapestry of Creation* was mentioned at the beginning of the 16th century for the last time and was obviously then removed. It was rediscovered in the 19th century in the attic of the cathedral. Today the partly restored *Creation Tapestry* is shown as a unique masterpiece of medieval art in the museum of the cathedral in Gerona.

To discover the symbolic meaning of the rich iconography of the *Creation Tapestry* opens up an insight in the common background of all religions back to the roots of shamanism, which use mandalas in dance as well as in images. To create or meditate mandalas is till today a healing process and affects the human psyche deeply. Mandalas enforce the tendencies to unite the opposites, which is so crucial in our time.

INTRODUCTION
TO THE TAPESTRY

The Gothic Cathedral of Gerona towers above the silhouette of the surrounding medieval town.[1] Compared to the baroque façade it is unadorned but imposing nevertheless, it is still one of the largest single-nave churches. Today, the adjoining monastery buildings to the north incorporate, among other things, the impressive Romanesque cloister, including half of the tower that is a part of it (both of which are dedicated to Charles the Great), along with the Romanesque side-chapel of "El Pedro."[2] The monastery buildings were once a part of the medieval ramparts of the city.[3] In the chapter house is a small museum that houses works of art from the Cathedral's treasury. Here, in a room of its own, hangs the "Tapís de la Creatió." The Creation Tapestry dates from the second half of the 11th century and is one of the oldest tapestries in Europe, comparable only to the Bayeux Tapestry.[4]

The Creation Tapestry, which is mounted on a beige piece of linen measuring approximately 380 cm by 420 cm, is displayed in simple surroundings with soft lighting. Until recently, only a low, inconspicuous, glass barrier separated the viewer from the electronically-guarded Tapestry, enabling one to have an immediate

---

[1] Girona is the Catalan spelling. In official Castilian Spanish, it is written as Gerona. Gerona is the capital city (pop. 99,000) of the north-eastern province of the same name to which the Costa Brava (wild coast) belongs, and it is the episcopal see of Gerona's bishopric.
[2] This Romanesque church was consecrated in 1038. The Gothic interior of the church was completed by 1604 and the Baroque façade by 1733.
[3] Gerona was a Celtic-Iberian settlement that was fortified in the Age of the Romans; it became Arabic in 713, but was re-conquered for a short time by Charlemagne in 785 and from the 9th century onward, it remained firmly in Christian hands. In 1809, Gerona withstood a seven-month siege by 35,000 men of the Napoleonic army.
[4] The Bayeux Tapestry (France) is thought to date from the second half of the 11th century. It is a 70 x 0.5 m long wall tapestry (embroidery on linen) that vividly depicts, in sequence, the Norman conquest of England, which began in 1064, by William the Conqueror.

experience of this medieval work of art. Nowadays, the glass barrier extends from floor to ceiling, providing more effective protection of such a unique object.

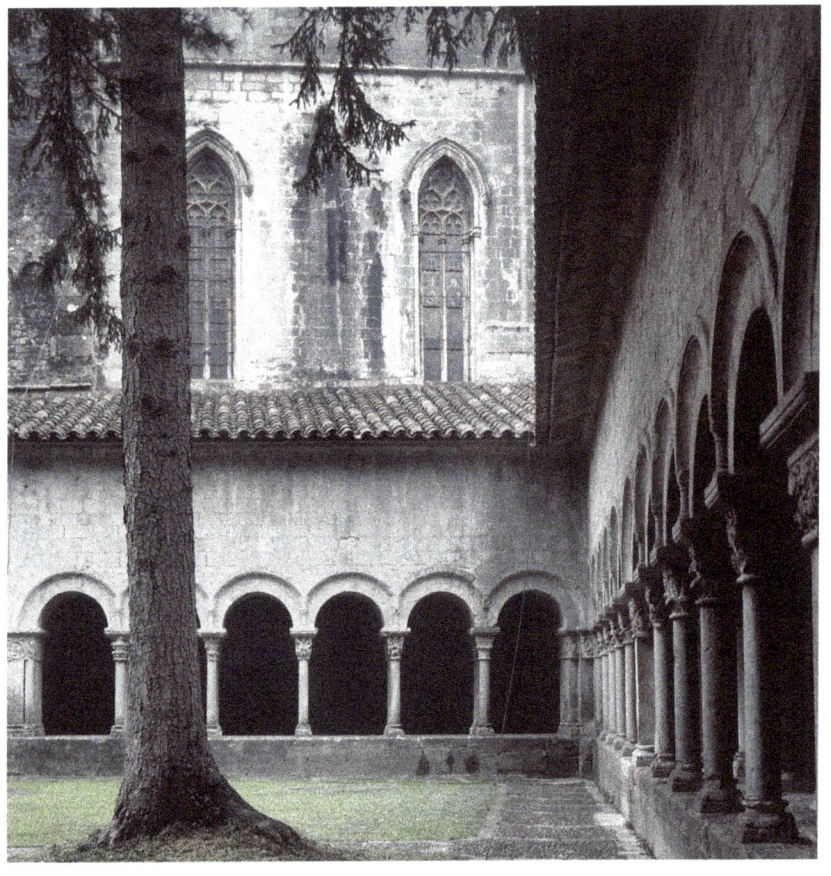

Each year, thousands of visitors come to view the Tapestry. Some show interest or astonishment, while others are moved or affected by it. Only a few are overwhelmed. The age-old images of the Tapestry express an eternal reality. Reality, however, is that which has an effect, that is, it is what happens in the here and now. Next to me, an elderly man makes mocking remarks in a loud voice about the primitive character of the Tapestry and then collapses from heart pain. Most people become silent as they gaze at the Tapestry and express their appreciation in whispers.

Eternal truths can only be expressed in man's contemporary creative endeavors. But everything we create ages and, as the context within which a work of art was created also fades, the eternal meaning it once held can only be surmised.

"Everything young grows old, all beauty fades, all heat cools, all brightness dims, and every truth becomes stale and trite. For all these things take on shape, and all shapes are worn thin by the working of time; they age, sicken, crumble to dust—unless they change. But change they can, for the invisible spark that generated them is potent enough for infinite generation. Yet every descent is followed by an ascent; the vanishing shapes are shaped anew, and a truth is valid in the end only if it suffers change and bears new witness in new images, in new tongues, like a new wine that is put into new bottles."[5]

In this sense, I felt forced to undertake this dangerous and laborious descent. I tried to stay alert as I made my descent, to brighten the ancient images with "the invisible spark of eternal creativity," and, in my own words and in my own way, to apprehend all that is fascinating in the Creation Tapestry. To what extent I have succeeded in this endeavor remains for the reader and the viewer of the Tapestry to decide. It is his or her *own* emotional response that will determine both the nature of, and the degree to which, this spark of eternal creation will be lit within his or her *own* soul.

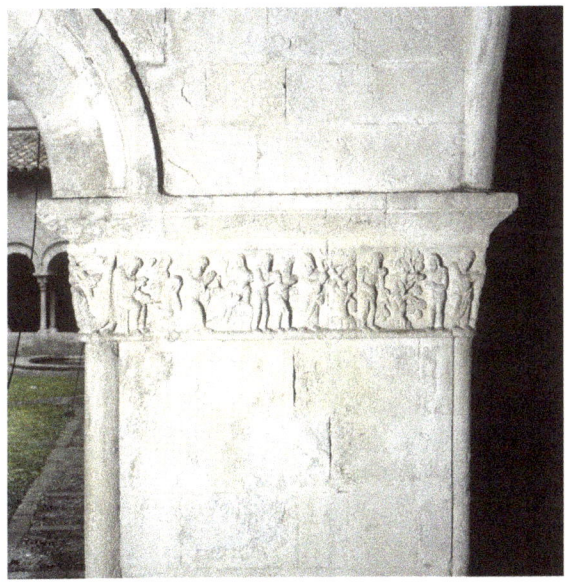 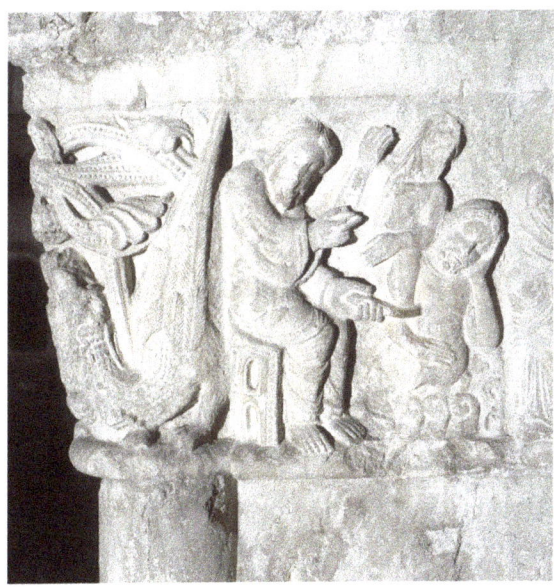

The aim of this book is to pick up the threads where Pedro de Palol, one of the greatest experts on the Tapestry, finished his distinguished work, *Une Broderie Catalane* with the following remark: "Nothing would be of greater interest in the study of the Creation Tapestry of Girona, than to discover the symbolic

---

[5] Jung, *Symbols of Transformation*, vol. 5, *CW*, § 553.

meaning of its rich iconography, to be able to explain the intensions of the authors."[6] In order to understand the symbolic content to which he refers, I have used the method of amplification which C. G. Jung employs in numerous publications[7] and which has been used since by various authors, following Jung's example.[8] This method involves selecting motifs from the history of civilization, motifs which share the same or a similar meaning as the symbol to be interpreted, and thereby reach an understanding of the symbol. A symbol, however, can never be fully explained. It is invariably more than the sum of any interpretation given to it. If this were not so, a symbol would simply remain a designation for something known, like a signpost.

In every era and, as Jung writes, "at every new stage in the differentiation of consciousness to which civilisation attains, with the task of finding a new *interpretation* appropriate to this stage, in order to connect the life of the past that still exists in us with the life of the present, which threatens to slip away from it. If this link-up does not take place, a kind of rootless consciousness comes into being, no longer oriented to the past, a consciousness which succumbs helplessly to all manner of suggestions and, in practice, is susceptible to psychic epidemics. With the loss of the past, now become 'insignificant,' devalued and incapable of revaluation, the saviour is lost too, for the saviour is either the insignificant thing itself or else arises out of it."[9]

When dealing with historical and art-historical facts, my work is based upon the small amount of academic study which has been done in this area.[10] Despite extensive scientific research, however, the history of the Tapestry and the use to which it was put remain unclear. Consequently, it has been my conscious intention not to endorse all the speculation and hypothesizing which has taken place up to the present. Rather, I have

---

[6] Palol, "Une broderie catalane," 246. (Translated by the author)
[7] For example, from Jung's *Collected Works*: *Aion*, vol. 9/II, *Mysterium Coniunctionis*, vol. 14, *Psychology and Alchemy*, vol. 12, *Psychology and Religion*, vol. 11, *Symbols of Transformation*, vol. 5.
[8] For example, von Franz, *Interpretation of Fairy Tales, Number and Time, Passion of Perpetua*; Isler, *Sennenpuppe*; Etter, *Felix und Regula, Einsiedler Meinrad*.
[9] Jung, *Archetypes*, vol. 9/I, *CW*, § 267.
[10] Of particular importance is the publication of the monography *El Tapíz de la Creació de la Catedral de Girona* by Pedro de Palol in 1986 that outlines the research he has done on the Tapestry over decades. It is in Catalan Spanish. For this reason, I asked to meet with him in person in 1988 to discuss his latest findings and thoughts on the Tapestry, and to hear more about his unpublished hypotheses on the Tapestry. I shall reference this discussion in footnotes that follow: Palol, private discussion (pd).

tried to find a new way of understanding this magnificent collection of images by using my own insights as my guide. Because of this, my arguments are not primarily of an historical or art-historical nature. More often they relate to the archetypal patterns of human creativity, that is, to patterns of the human collective psyche which have general validity. These patterns always reveal themselves initially in images.

My conclusions, therefore, should be seen in conjunction with, rather than instead of, current opinion. However, as they include the realm of sentiment or feeling, they exceed the confines of a purely scientific approach. Because what the Tapestry tells us is essentially of a religious and psychological nature, a purely scientific approach can render only a partial insight. This fact does not detract from the validity of such an approach but, because of its methodology, such an approach is necessarily more limited.

While visiting Barcelona, a remark made by Palol prompted me to reconsider Arabian influence upon the Creation Tapestry even though my manuscript was, in essence, already finished. At the time, he spoke of his unshakeable conviction that the Tapestry had absolutely nothing to do with either Arabian culture or with Islam as the Tapestry embodied not a single iconographic allusion to Arabian art. With this in mind, he came to the conclusion that the Tapestry could not have been made on Spanish soil. Such a strictly art-historical argument seems to me to carry little conviction. On the contrary, it is my belief that the very fact that the Christian God in the tapestry is represented within the framework of a mandala points toward a strong connection to Islam, for it is within Islam that the mandala is *the* accepted form for representation of the divine. In addition, the very fact that we are dealing with a Creation *Tapestry* lends weight to assuming Arabian influence as tapestries began to appear in Europe only after contact had been made with Asian cultures.

Some of Islam's most respected mystics were born on Spanish soil, for example Ibn Masarra (of Cordoby, died 931) and Ibn Abbad Ar-Rondi (of Ronda, died 1390), but above all, the "Magister Magnum," Ibn 'Arabi (of Murcia, died 1240) whose prolific writings are believed by most Sufis to represent the ultimate in mystical revelation. There is evidence that Christian scholars made their first contact with Sufi ideas as early as the Middle Ages. In the writings of the great Catalan mystic, poet, and philosopher Ramon Lull (Raimundus

Lullus,1235–1316), there are already clear indications of his preoccupation with mystical Arabian literature.[11] One can also recognize Islamic influence in certain ideas of St. John of the Cross (1542–1591), who was an important religious scholar, mystic, and poet for Spain.[12] Thus, I have tried to trace Islamic influence in the Creation Tapestry above all with regard to content rather than to iconography. Such parallel references to Islam in general, and to Sufism in particular, I have woven into the conclusion of this manuscript.

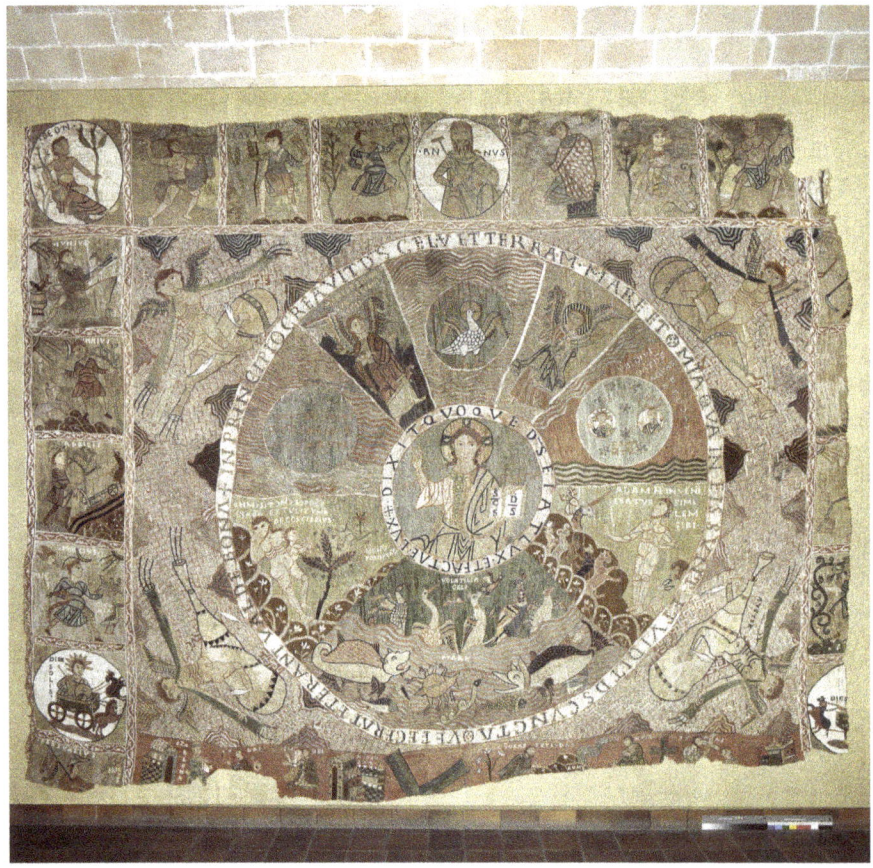

Once my attempt to interpret the imagery of the Tapestry was finished, I felt the urge to try to reconstruct the missing fragments of the Tapestry, not just in a schematic way, but rather as true to the original as possible. It should only be seen as a tentative attempt to see how the fragment fitted into the context of the whole Tapestry. If my reconstruction, which is based on strong evidence, inspires further thought, it will have achieved its purpose.

---

[11] Schimmel, *Mystical Dimensions of Islam*, 7–8.

[12] Ibid., 253. The concept of the "Dark Night of the Soul" in the work of St. John of the Cross and of Ibn Abbad is particularly comparable; it refers to a state in which one's ego is surrendered and the mystic only acts in accordance with the directives he perceives to come from God.

DESCRIPTION OF THE TAPESTRY

Originally, the Tapestry measured approximately 5 x 5 m.[13] On each of its four sides, eight squares form a frame around a central circular representation of the Creation. Below this circle, in rectangular form, is a depiction of the legend of St. Helena, which also forms part of its framework.

Moving upward from the bottom left-hand corner and with strict symmetry between the right and left sides, the first six months of the year are depicted. January is no longer there, and February exists only as a fragment. Between February and March, the chariot of the sun has been inserted. Moving downward from the top right-hand corner, are the second group of six months. Only fragments of some of these months remain today, with November and December missing altogether. Between October and November, the chariot of the moon has been inserted.

Each month depicts a man who is engaged in work appropriate to the time of year, all of whom are facing the center of the Tapestry. January: unknown; February: a man is carrying dead birds hanging from a staff over his shoulder; March: a man, together with a snake, toad, and stork (CIGONIA); April: a man is tilling the ground with a plough pulled by two horses; May: a man is feeding a horse in a field; June: a man is depicted as a bird catcher and fisherman; July: a man is harvesting with a scythe; August: a man is cutting corn with a sickle; September: a man is threshing grain with a flail; October: a man is harvesting grapes with a vintner's knife (VINEA); November: unknown; December: unknown. From the upper corners of each

---

[13] This refers to the assumption that it had a square format, a hypothesis that is supported by many arguments (see Chapter: The Tapestry as a Mandala). While Palol does not exclude the possibility of the Tapestry having a square format (Palol, *El Tapíz de la Creació*, Fig. 60, 74), he suggests it had a "double-square" format of approximately 5 x 10 m (pd); cf. ibid., Fig. 62, 76; and see here footnote (fn) 30.

picture there is either a cool wind blowing (FRICUS) or a warm sun shining (SOL), depending on the time of year.

At the top of the Tapestry, enthroned in the middle, is ANNUS, a divine personification of the year, holding the wheel of time and a tool. From left to right, he is surrounded by the four seasons. In summer: a man is harvesting grain with a scythe; autumn: a man is cutting grapes with a vintner's knife; winter: a man wrapped in fur is sitting on a stool, warming himself by a fire; spring: a man is tilling soil with a spade. In summer, the sun is shining (ESTAS, FLAX). In autumn (AUTUMNUS), nuts (NUX) are ripening. In winter (HIEMS), cold winds (FRICUS) are blowing and fire (IGNIS) gives warmth. In spring too, a cold wind (FRICUS) is still blowing. On either side of the four illustrations of the seasons is a representation of scenes from the story of Samson from the Book of Judges in the Old Testament (Chapters 13–16). On the left, Samson (SAMSON) is swinging the jaw-bone of an ass, ready to slay thousands of Philistines. On the right, he is about to cut a honeycomb from the carcass of a lion.[14]

The four pictures in the four corners of the Tapestry depict the four rivers of paradise. In each, a man is holding onto the tree of eternal life, which grows in the center of paradise, while pouring water from an antique vessel. In the top left-hand corner is Gihon (Geon). It is probable that the Pison, Euphratis, and Tigris rivers are depicted in the other three corners.[15]

All of these pictures, which together make up the framework of the Tapestry, are surrounded by a border of undulating vines clinging to narrow red bands. Taken together, these images represent everyday medieval life which was ruled by the eternal cycle of the seasons and by the rhythmical progression of the sun and the moon in the course of a year, which was the largest, all-encompassing natural unit of time.

Everyday life, limited as it is by space and time, is allowed to expand to the very edge of the world where gigantic mountains rise up. As in a child's drawing, these mountains are depicted as striped triangles positioned at right angles to the border and to the inner circle. Beyond them, and beyond space and time,

---

[14] Palol does not see this image as a further depiction from the Samson legend. He believes the skin to be that of a sheep, referencing Abel and the sacrificial lamb, but he has not reached any satisfactory conclusion (pd); cf. Palol, *El Tapíz de la Creació*, 26ff. and ill. 36.

[15] This fragment of the upper-right corner image is symmetrical to the better-preserved image in the upper-left corner.

eternity begins. Here begins the Kingdom of God. Between these two realms blow the eternal winds out of the four cardinal points. In the lower right-hand corner is the Wind of the South (AUSTER). Diametrically opposite in the top left-hand corner is the Wind of the North (SEPTENTRIO). In the lower left-hand corner is the Wind of the West (CEPHIRUS) and opposite it, in the top right-hand corner, is the Wind of the East (SUBSOLANUS). These winds are shown as pagan Wind Gods, riding on air-filled skin bags out of which the winds flow. In addition, each Wind God is blowing through two pipes. Only the Wind God of the East, sitting upon his puckered wind sack, is not blowing.

These flying wind-demons are set against a background of a finely-interwoven network of strictly geometrical scroll-like patterns, which unite the eternal realm with everyday life in infinite diversity.

The outer circle, which constitutes the beginning of the realm of the eternal, consists of a white band upon which the following text is inscribed (beginning from center left): "IN PRINCIPIO CREAVIT DEUS CELUM ET TERRAM MARE ET OMNIA QUE IN EIS SUNT ET VIDIT DEUS CUNCTA QUE FECERAT ET ERANT VALDE BONA" (In the beginning, God created Heaven and Earth, the Sea and all that there is therein, and saw all He had created and saw that it was good.)

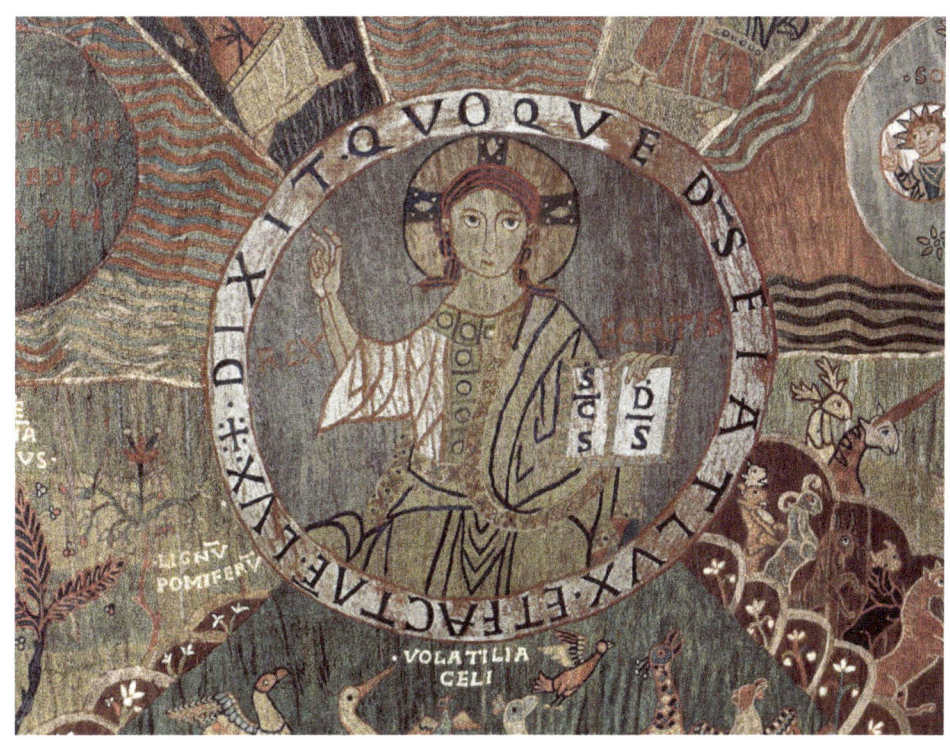

"The tapestry comprises such a number of archetypal images and relationships, that a participation from the collective unconscious seems likely. The composition owes its layout as well as its intuitive content to the archetypal influences.

The image is equal to a revelation or better, can be valued as a reworking of traditional religious concepts in a form which corresponds to the very essence of medieval natural philosophy, and thus a structure of the unconscious."

The above is a commentary by C. G. Jung on a tapestry depicting "the Sermon of the Mount," which had been given to him for his 70th birthday. (A short essay about the tapestry in: M. Ruetschi, *Die Bergpredigt: Kindern in Bildern erzählt, nach einem Wandteppich von Rosa Gerber*, with an introduction by C. G. Jung (Freiburg i.B.: Herder, 1988), 30–31. Translated by Kappes)

The innermost circle is also bordered by a white band upon which the following text is inscribed: "DIXIT QUOQUE DEUS, FIAT LUX ET FACTA EST LUX" (And God said, let there be light and there was light.) In the center of the Tapestry is the Creator seated on a throne and wearing a white embroidered garment with a loose-fitting robe draped over His left shoulder. In His left hand, He is holding an open book with the abbreviated inscription "SANCTUS DEUS" (Holy God), while His right hand is raised in a gesture of benediction. Horizontally running across the middle of this circle, and barely legible are the words "REX FORTIS" (Mighty King)

In the upper middle of the outer circle, a smaller blue circle is surrounded by primordial waters. Within this circle is a dove with colored wings and a white body around which is the barely legible inscription: "SPIRITUS DEI FEREBATUR SUPER AQUAS" (The Spirit of God moved over the waters). The reddish-blue wavy lines that fill the circle represent the water. A shining halo divided into four segments encircles the head of the dove, a detail which the dove shares with the Creator at the center of the Tapestry.

In the symmetrical segments on either side of the dove, God's labors on the first day of creation are depicted. On the left is an angel with colored wings wearing a long, yellow robe and a red outer garment. The angel is holding an extinguished torch. He has no halo. Above him is written: "TENEBRE ERANT SUPER FACIEM ABISSI" (Darkness lay over the waters). Darkness is suggested by the dark background. On the right is an angel with colored wings wearing a blue outer garment over a slightly shorter red robe. He is floating in front of a light background, his head surrounded by a halo. He personifies light: "LUX" (Light).

Below the picture on the left depicting darkness is the second day of creation. This segment, too, is filled with reddish-blue wavy lines signifying primordial waters. Within it floats a blue circle bearing the inscription: "FECIT DEUS FIRMAMENTUM IN MEDIO AQUARUM" (God created the firmament in the middle of the waters).

Opposite this segment, on the right-hand side, the third and fourth days of creation are depicted. At the top and bottom of this segment are the wavy reddish-blue lines of the divided waters, between which a blue circle floats on a red background. Within this circle are two smaller white circles in which the male sun (SOL) with his many-pointed halo and the female moon (LUNA) with her crescent moon and six stars (FIRMAMENTUM), are depicted, making eight celestial bodies in all. On the right-hand side of this segment is written: "UBI DIVIDAT DEUS AQUAS AB AQUIS" (Where God divided the water from the waters).

In the lower half of this larger outer circle the creation of animate nature is represented. The middle segment of this lower half depicts the labor of the fifth day of creation: the fishes of the sea (CETE GRANDIA: big fishes; MARE: sea) and the birds of the sky (VOLATILIA CELI: birds of the sky).

The segment to the right of this depiction of animate nature shows the sixth day of creation, the day in which the creatures of the earth, here the animals of the woods and fields, were created along with the first human being, Adam, who was made in God's image. While searching for more of his own kind, Adam is depicted, shaken and defensive, naming the animals which surround him: of the domestic animals, he gives name to the horse, cow, goat, sheep, dog, and cat; of the wild animals, the stag and unicorn are named. Two mythical animals stand threateningly behind him. The text reads: "ADAM NON INVENIEBATUR SIMILEM SIBI" (Adam did not find any creature of his own kind).

The eighth and final segment on the left in the lower half of the circle is also based upon the second story of creation. Here, after having put a reclining Adam into a deep sleep, God removes one of Adam's ribs out of which Eve, the first human female, is formed. This scene is depicted as taking place next to the tree of eternal life, which grows in the center of paradise. Beside it also stands the tree of knowledge, of good and evil (LIGNUM POMIFERUM: fruit tree). The text gives a short explanation: "INMISIT DOMINUS SOPOREM IN ADAM ET TULIT UNAM DE COSTIS EIUS" (God put Adam into a deep sleep and removed one of his ribs).

In the lower fragmented edge of the Tapestry, set against a red background, events from the legend of St. Helena, mother of Constantine the Great, as well as the finding of the Holy Cross of Christ are shown. Going from left to right, one can only just recognise the following scenes: in front of a church, Saint Helena (SANCTA ELENA) is in conversation with a Jew (JUDAS); behind this scene, two Jews (JUDEI) stand in front of a church in Jerusalem (HIERUSAL); in the center of the picture, a tilting cross, under the short right-hand arm of which is a decorative cross on top of a gem-encrusted crown, most probably the crown of Constantine the Great[16], (the son of Saint Helena); there is also a flowering tree; a man praying in a field (CUM ORASSET JUDAS: as Judas prayed) through which a brook is flowing (EUMUS: earth); Judas digging with a spade (JUDAS); two upright crosses; Judas in front of a church holding a cross over a kneeling Jew.[17]

---

[16] Palol reached this interesting conclusion after making extensive comparisons: Palol, *El Tapíz de la Creació*, 130–31; and Palol, "Une broderie catalane." 244.
[17] Cf. Palol, "Une broderie catalane"; Calzada, "El mosaic de Beth-Alpha."

THE HISTORY OF THE TAPESTRY

Most of the papers written about the Creation Tapestry have been published in Spanish and some, particularly the more recent ones, have been published in Catalan. Information relevant to our discussion has been taken and summarized from these papers. Most scholars and experts agree that the Creation Tapestry was made in the late 11th or early 12th century. Bernat Humbert was the influential Bishop of Gerona from 1094 to 1111. In 1097, during his time in office, a Church Council was held and the Romanesque cathedral was completed. The building had been started by Bishop Pere de Rotger de Carcassona and was inaugurated in 1038 before being completed. It would seem that the cathedral had three naves and three apses built around the choir. Next to the main entrance was a chapel—"El Sepulcre"—first mentioned in 1106, with an altar of the Holy Cross.[18]

Although the place and time of the origin of the Tapestry are not known with absolute certainty, it would seem that it was made in Catalonia[19], on Spanish Christian soil, probably around 1100 in Gerona itself where an important scriptorium existed at the time.[20] The high quality of the work indicates that its creator must have been an expert on classical antiquity who must have had access to Byzantine and Carolingian manuscripts from which he drew his inspiration and which served as his model.[21]

---

[18] Marqués, "El Tapíz," 217–18.
[19] Mundo, "L'escriptura del Tapíz," 158.
[20] Ibid.; and Calzada, "El mosaic de Beth-Alpha," 202.
[21] Palol, "Une broderie catalane," 250. Today, he is rather of the opinion that the Tapestry was created in northern Italy, in response to a contract received from or for Gerona. Upon its completion – shortly before 1100 – it was immediately used in the cathedral of Gerona (pd); cf. also Palol, *El Tapíz de la Creació*, 154.

Reference was made to the Tapestry for the first time in 1538. Oddly enough, the Tapestry was never mentioned prior to this date, even in the inventories of the Cathedral.[22] However, King Charles V (1500–1558) visited the Bishop of Gerona, and he revisited the church in order to see the "tapestry of Charlemagne with the story of Emperor Constantine."[23]

It is not surprising that the Tapestry is referred to in this manner in the itinerary of the king's visit, for the Cathedral had been dedicated to Charlemagne (742–814). It was Charlemagne, the Frankish king, who, by mounting a brave campaign, had liberated the Spanish borderlands beyond Barcelona from 100 years of Muslim domination.

Although the Tapestry already existed by 1100, the first official record of it was made only in 1538. This fact may lend weight to the idea that throughout the Middle Ages, the Tapestry was in the possession of a group of Christian esoterics. If this were so, the general public would not have had access to the Tapestry and it was, in fact, only from the 16th century onward that it could be seen in the Cathedral of Gerona. Furthermore, it is also possible to imagine that the Tapestry was only on show at certain celebrations and on special occasions.[24]

After the completion of the Gothic Cathedral (1604), it would appear that the Tapestry was removed and was rediscovered and put on display again only in the last century. Two restorations of the Tapestry were then undertaken between 1880–1884, and between 1900–1910. In 1952, the Tapestry underwent further extensive restoration and in 1975, the representation of the month of April was supplemented.[25] It is in this form that the Tapestry is shown today in the Chapter House of the Cathedral. After its restoration, academic interest in the Tapestry was aroused. Since the end of the last century, numerous monographs have been published.[26] In addition, in 1980, the magazine *Revista de Gerona* devoted an entire issue (Vol. 92) to the Tapestry.[27]

---

[22] Palol, "Une broderie catalane," 192.

[23] Battle, "El brodat de la Creació," 212–13.

[24] Palol is decidedly against this possibility (pd).

[25] Battle, "El brodat de la Creació," 214.

[26] Girbal, "Tapiz notable de la Catedral"; Kendrick, "Textiles"; Martinell, "El tesoro artistico de Cataluniã"; Gudiol, *Els primitius*; Font, "El Tapiz de la Creación"; Pijoan, *Summa Artis*; Palol, "Une broderie catalane"; and Palol, *El Tapíz de la Creació*.

[27] On 25.10.1980 (first day of issue) the Spanish Post issued a series of postage stamps depicting the Tapestry: three stamps for 25 Pesetas

There has been some discussion about the possibility that the very fragmented part of the Tapestry which deals with the story of the finding of the Holy Cross may have existed as a separate wall-hanging which was then added to the Creation Tapestry at a later date. There is, however, no evidence from the sewing, embroidering or weaving techniques used on the Tapestry to support such a theory. Moreover, the fact that the Tapestry has an apparent square form speaks against such a hypothesis.[28]

Some regard the Creation Tapestry as being merely a means to popularise religious teachings,[29] and one might view the religious texts woven into the Tapestry as being an argument to uphold this view. In my opinion, however, at least some of these texts could have been added at some later date for it can be assumed that over the centuries, the direct impact of the Tapestry diminished and single words, groups of words and sentences were then embroidered into the Tapestry to make its meaning more accessible to both the clergy and to laymen.[30] Most of the authors who have expressed an opinion about the meaning of the Tapestry have come to the conclusion that its central statement has its roots in Genesis, the First Book of Moses (in the Old Testament), as well as in Paul's epistle to the Colossians (New Testament, Chapters 15–20): Jesus Christ is the center of the universe and of history; He is the Pantocrator, the Cronocrator, and the Cosmocrator, He is the Lord, our God, the King of Kings. In addition, by his passion and his crucifixion, he shows mankind the way back to paradise.[31]

However, none of the authors take the trouble of substantiating their opinions, presumably in the belief that the facts are self-evident and any explanation is therefore superfluous. Without wishing to challenge their attempts at a hypothesis in any basic way, I must, however, state that I do not share this opinion. Because the Creation Tapestry displays such a wealth of symbolism in its geometric design and construction, in its composition of figures and color, in its numbers and movement, in its various motifs and scenes and in its biblical texts, it does, in fact, surpass such a hypothesis. The Tapestry conveys a comprehensive pictorial

---

(upper row) and 3 stamps for 50 Pesetas (lower row) in a first edition of 6 million copies.
[28] Battle, "El brodat de la Creació," 214–15.
[29] Taberner, *El Tapíz.*
[30] Palol does not believe any later additions of this kind were made (pd).
[31] Palol, "Une broderie catalane," 246ff; Camprodon, "Pòrtic," 149.

synopsis of the cosmological view of the world at that time. This view became increasingly incomprehensible over the course of the centuries until finally, the Tapestry and what it represents were completely forgotten.[32]

Today, the Creation Tapestry is once again on show, but only as a remarkable and unique art-historical example of its kind. For most people, its eternally valid content remains hidden, although in many, if not all, of the people who view it, inexplicably deep feelings are aroused, feelings which are rooted in the archetypal nature of the Tapestry's images. In this way, it is possible for a viewer to get an inkling of his own mysterious connection to the flow of eternal images in the collective unconscious. Bearing this in mind, the present paper does not in any way lay claim to attempting a complete interpretation of the Tapestry. There is always more to an image than any interpretation can render, and my goal will have been achieved if the reader of this book and the viewer of the Tapestry come closer to the stream of eternally valid images in his *own* soul. For this reason, all historical, art-historical and iconographical viewpoints will be kept in the background for they have been dealt with at length elsewhere (see above and bibliography).

---

[32] Palol sees all Christian thought framed between Genesis and the Apocalypse, with its kernel being the story of Christ's Redemption. In his view, the Tapestry can reflect only this content. Because it is without a single reference to the Apocalypse, in a formal reconstruction, he adds a second square to the "lower" half – thereby doubling the size of the Tapestry – that references only the Apocalypse. He would like to see the frame expanded by including the signs of the zodiac (pd).

ON THE USE OF THE TAPESTRY

Working on a piece of linen which was undoubtedly stretched to cover a rectangular frame, the ornamental features and figures of the Tapestry were embroidered in colored wool, using two different stitching techniques.[33] For years, if not decades, many men and women worked on the Tapestry following a detailed plan in order to complete it, and then to mend damaged areas and, as mentioned above, to add written explanations of the images which were deemed necessary as time went by. Judging by the clear concept and homogeneous composition of the Tapestry, it must have been designed by one individual. But the many hands which created the Tapestry, which added, omitted or gave an accent to some detail combined to make the Tapestry not only the work of an individual, but a collective achievement, as well.

The Creation Tapestry must never have been used as a floor covering for its work is too fine and well-preserved for such a purpose. Thus, most authors believe it was used perhaps as a canopy, or as a wall hanging behind an altar, or as an altar cloth. The idea of it being used as a catafalque cover has even been mentioned.[34]

The chronicler of King Charles V mentions the "Tapestry of Charlemagne, with the history of Emperor Constantine" in his writings. These images, set against a red background, more readily drew one's attention at that time than the actual history of creation as depicted in the other two thirds of the Tapestry. This casual remark leads me to the following hypothesis: that the major part of the Tapestry depicting the history of creation was used as a canopy above the altar while the lower third, with the legend of the finding of the

---

[33] González, "Dos tapíces," 166–67.

[34] Palol, "Une broderie catalane"; Calzada, "El mosaic de Beth-Alpha"; Marqués, "El Tapíz." Palol prefers the idea of it being used as a catafalque for an important, though still unknown personage who died shortly before 1100 in Gerona (pd).

Holy Cross by St. Helena, hung behind the altar. Used in this way, the lower part of the Tapestry would have provided a perfect thematic embellishment to the Holy Cross altar in the Romanesque "El Sepulcre" chapel, near to the main entrance of the Cathedral.[35] Or, perhaps the Tapestry was hung in the Romanesque side-chapel "El Pedro," or in the chancel of the Cathedral. In a semi-circular chancel, a square-shaped canopy would not seem to be harmonious, whereas a rectangular canopy would appear to fit.

Acceptance of this hypothesis helps to explain a detail which has not received any special attention up to the present time, that is, the Tapestry is damaged mostly at its edges, especially at the top, on the right-hand side and on its lower edge. If it had been hung as a wall-hanging, its considerable weight would lead to damage being done mostly along its upper edge, not along the right, left or bottom edge. The Creation Tapestry is, however, mostly damaged along its upper, its left-hand and especially its right-hand edge, as well as along the border between the history of creation images, and the depiction of the Legend of the Holy Cross. Therefore, if the Tapestry was indeed hung as described above, that is, as both a canopy and as a wall-hanging simultaneously, its damaged borders correspond with the lines which would have been subjected to the greatest force of gravity.

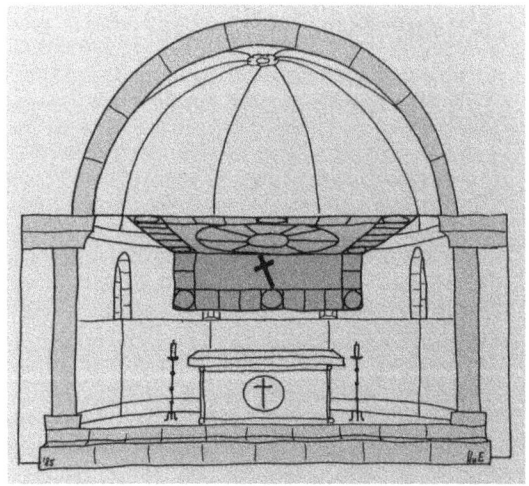

Was the Creation Tapestry replaced by the embossed silver canopy which spans the high altar up to the present day, even before 1362, when the Gothic cathedral was under construction? This silver canopy is rectangular and its size approximates the size of what remains of the Creation Tapestry. In addition, the silver canopy is slightly arched and is drawn in at the sides in a manner meant to suggest a cloth canopy. At its center is the Coronation of Mary which, in some respects, brings together all the different aspects of the Creation Tapestry (see the chapters "The Meaning of the Tapestry," and "The Creation Tapestry, a Catalan Canopy").

---

[35] Marqués, "El Tapíz," 221.

THE MEANING OF THE TAPESTRY

A. Its Meaning as a Tapestry

Carpets only became known in Europe after contact had been made with Asia and its culture. In medieval Spain, cultural exchange flourished with Arab immigration. For nomadic Arabian tribes, their skilfully woven carpets, upon which their camps were made each evening, ensured a connection to the earth of their homeland. Their carpets gave them the feeling that they had familiar, rather than foreign, earth beneath their feet safeguarding them from the inimical influences of foreign soil. Their carpets were tantamount to the native soil upon which they had been raised, a place where they felt at home within a hostile environment.[36] For this reason, carpets are endowed with feminine qualities.

If a carpet can be viewed as being a piece of one's homeland which protects one from foreign soil, then, in quite the same way, a canopy can be viewed as being a protection from strange and hostile influences from above. A canopy can signify a spiritual home where one finds shelter from foreign ideas and influences. Like a roof which protects one from the extremities of weather, from thunder and lightning, from wind and rain, a canopy can keep out strange ideas which might take the form of menacing thoughts, disturbing fantasies, or inspirations that seem threatening as they do not belong to one's own spiritual background. As in a covered four-poster bed, where the canopy protects the bedding from dust and dirt filtering down, the Creation Tapestry provides protection from threatening spiritual infiltration.

---

[36] Von Franz, *Interpretation of Fairy Tales*, 75–76.

The historical circumstances prevalent in northeastern Spain at the time reveal the nature of this spiritual menace. The northern Spanish borderlands, which were separated from Christian Europe by the Pyrenees, were under continuous threat of being overrun by Islamic forces, which had ruled three-quarters of the Iberian Peninsula for centuries. On the one hand, such Islamic influence was enormously fruitful for the furtherment of European culture. It brought with it much of the spiritual wisdom of classical antiquity, which had been translated by the Arabs and further developed by them, and this influence proved to be long-lasting. On the other hand, the Mohammedans were determined to do battle with the Christians with the motto: convert or die.

The mystical tradition of Sufism demonstrates the high level of cultural differentiation of Islam in the late Middle Ages. In Sufism, the inner dimension of Islam is described in the experience of ecstatic visions by its mystics. The central aim of Sufism is to find one's *inner* path to knowledge until enlightenment is reached.[37] Some sources trace the beginnings of Sufism back to Mohammed. His story begins with his receival of the Quran from God.[38] Although they do not belong to the Koran itself, special importance is given to the Forty Sacred Traditions in which the Divine speaks through the Prophet in the first person singular. Other significant sources of doctrine include the Commentaries upon the Koran by individual Sufis, the Prophetic Traditions, the Books of Sayings of the Shi'ite imams, particularly those of Ali, the first Shi'ite imam, and the great treasury of Sufi poetry, above all, the Mathnawi of Jalaluddin Rumi, which has been described as a Persian commentary upon the Koran.[39]

At the time of the making of the Creation Tapestry, Sufism was flourishing, and its zenith was reached with the extensive writings of Ibn 'Arabi (born 1164 in Murcia, died 1240 in Damascus). He is regarded as being the most productive, imaginative, knowledgeable and far-seeing writer of Sufism.[40] There are at least 300 of his writings in existence, of which the *Book of Seals* (also known as *The Wisdom of the Prophets*) is the most highly respected. In it, one can find the quintessence of his school of thought, for it is here that, in a

---

[37] Bakhtiar, *Sufi*, 7.
[38] Ibid., 6.
[39] Ibid., 7.
[40] Cf. Ibn al 'Arabi, *Wisdom of the Prophets*, ix–xi.

mature manner, he defends the teaching of the Unity of Being. His writing is based on the Koran, but also on the Gnosis, the Stoa and the philosophy of Philos, the Jew, as well as on the writings of earlier Sufis.[41]

For a Muslim, his carpet signifies not only his own piece of mother earth, but the inner foundation of his whole life. As Mohammedans were not allowed to make any concrete image of their God, Allah, most of the mainly abstract pictorial elements of Arabian carpets are geometrical forms which are based upon religious concepts.[42] This explains why their God-image is often depicted by a mandala, rich in symbolism. For a Sufi, symbolism is the most respected of all sciences. In his view, symbols express realities already inherent in the nature of things. It is through symbols that a Sufi mystic is awakened and transformed. His entire journey toward God is undertaken in symbols and, through his interaction with the symbolic world, his awareness of the reality of things is continually increased. For it is the qualities of Divine Existence, of the imperceptible archetypal patterns, which become apparent through symbols, through archetypal images which are a part of the nature of all things. Whoever does not succeed in attaining this knowledge is in danger of drowning in a flood of unconscious forces. "Everything in creation is a symbol: for everything perceived by the *outer* senses may be conceived through the *inner* senses as a sign of a higher state of reality. However, this symbolic vision takes place, for the Sufi, only when the symbol is seen in the presence of the theophanic light."[43] This light cannot be seen as such, but rather it becomes visible by means of a symbol through whose form this light permeates.[44]

The Sufi differentiates between universal symbols, which form the basis of our human inheritance, and those special symbols which are linked to personal or collective traditions. The universal symbols, which can be found in Islamic art, especially in its architecture, music, and calligraphy, are a part of what is considered to be most profound in Sufism. They are derived from The Word which gives expression to Divine Names. They are shown in a dream whereupon the world of archaic images is revealed.[45] In this manner, they correspond exactly to what Jung termed "archetypal images" (see pages 26-27).

---

[41] Ibid.
[42] Von Franz, *Interpretation of Fairy Tales*, 77.
[43] Bakhtiar, *Sufi*, 27.
[44] Ibid., 26.
[45] Cf. Ibn al 'Arabi, *Wisdom of the Prophets*, 59–67.

In our own culture, too, we speak of "the web of fate" or "the rich tapestry of life," and, even in modern dreams, carpets take on this meaning.[46] The Spirit of the Earth in Part One of *Faust* states:

"So work I on the whirring loom of time, the life that clothes the deity sublime."[47]

Goethe presumably took this motif from the creation myth of Pherecydes, who refers to the earth as being a giant web spread out over the world oak tree.[48] The Creation Tapestry, then, can be seen as a symbol for the mysterious, divine web of fate, both for the individual as well as for the Christian community of the Spanish borderlands of the 11th and 12th centuries.

The town of Gerona in Spain lies at the junction of the two great cultures of the West, both of which were steeped in Jewish tradition. Accordingly, it was necessary for the people of Gerona to reflect upon their own spiritual standpoint. The Creation Tapestry as Canopy came to serve as a spiritual base and as a *terra firma* for it was viewed as a shelter of *Christian culture,* as a source of courage and strength and as a place where a Christian could find his bearings within the melting pot of the great Western cultures. It was not by chance that it was in Gerona that the powerful bishop Bernat Humberts called a Church Council in 1097. By the making of the Creation Tapestry, the Church created a further visible sign of both the strength and the power of Christianity on Spanish soil. The Tapestry depicts a comprehensive image of the Divine, as perceived by the Christian community of that time. In this way, the eternal truth, which cannot be grasped by reason alone, was thus expressed through the use of images.

To place oneself under the shelter of the Creation Canopy meant for a person of that time to be given the chance to re-align himself with the pattern of fate of the Christian tradition, to reflect again upon the God-image of that time, an image which determined the fate of the Christian community. And finally, it offered him the chance to see himself as being removed from the "aberrations" of Islam and Judaism, both of which can be seen to have had a fertilizing influence upon life in Gerona as it was then.

---

[46] For example, a man hides in the forest outside of Jerusalem that is under the occupation of the Arabs. If he manages to bring a tapestry, that he has in his possession, into the city, the latter will be freed.

[47] Goethe, *Dramen*, vol. 3, *Goethes Werke*, 501. (Translated by Kappes)

[48] Von Franz, *Interpretation of Fairy Tales*, 78; and von Franz, *Individuation in Fairy Tales*, 53: All the things that have been embroidered into the coat stretched over the earth correspond to the things that can be found in our world.

B. The Tapestry as a Mandala

Another factor which speaks in favor of viewing the Creation Tapestry of Gerona as a representation of the Divinity as conceived in medieval contemporary Christian Spain is the fact that the Tapestry displays all the characteristics of a mandala. The formal elements of a mandala include:[49]

- the squaring of the circle, with the circle being contained within the square
- the circle is divided by the spokes of a wheel
- the circle is shown as being in rotation (winds blowing)
- the center often lies within an inner circle
- the center is divided into four rays (quartered aureole of the Pantocrator)
- the basic number is four or a multiple of it.

The most significant mandalas are found in areas influenced by Tibetan Buddhism. They are used to further contemplation and meditation. They aid concentration by "narrowing down the psychic field of vision and restricting it to the center."[50] As a rule, a Buddhist mandala portrays Shiva, the One Existent, the Timeless in His perfect state, from whom all of creation emanates. Creation begins with the division of the opposites, which, in Shiva, are united. It is out of their division, and the resultant huge explosion of energy, that the diversity of the world comes about.[51] In Lamaistic literature, one finds instruction down to the last detail about how such a mandala is to be painted and how it is to be used. Form and color must be used according to tradition, and any variation must remain within fairly narrow limits. "The goal of contemplating the processes depicted in the mandala is that the yogi shall become inwardly aware of the deity. Through contemplation, he recognizes himself as God again, and thus returns from the illusion of individual existence into the universal totality of the divine state."[52]

---

[49] Jung, *Archetypes*, vol. 9/I, *CW*, § 646.
[50] Ibid., § 630.
[51] Ibid., §§ 630–31.
[52] Ibid., § 633.

In Dervish monasteries, mandalas are also a dance form and they can be found as far back as Palaeolithic times in the form of simple scratchings or drawings on rock faces and on stones. In medieval alchemy, mandalas were known as "squaring the circle," for they represented the synthesis of the four elements, which forever strive to separate.[53] As a psychological phenomenon, they appear spontaneously in the dreams and fantasies or paintings of modern man which permits further study of their functional meaning. As a rule, mandalas are spontaneous manifestations of the unconscious which surface in conditions of psychic dissociation or disorientation. When such a condition is present, unintelligible contents from the unconscious disrupt a person's conscious life and he becomes increasingly confused. In such a moment of disorientation, the strict and orderly pattern of a mandala compensates the disorder of the psychic state of the individual, for it imposes a concentric pattern upon the asymmetrical contents, and brings all into relationship with the center.[54]

The unintelligible contents that posed a threat to Christianity at the time had their origins in classical antiquity and in the cultural heritages of both Islam and Judaism, both of which had a creative influence upon Christianity, despite the fact that Christianity was under attack from both religions, especially from the Muslims.

As our comparative study shows, when a mandala arises, a fundamental pattern, a so-called archetype, is activated which can be found universally and which does not owe its individual existence to any one tradition. Accordingly, though individual mandalas may vary greatly in design, as well as in the time and place of their origin, nevertheless they share a basic similarity behind which the "archetype of wholeness" can be recognized.[55]

What do we mean by the term "archetype"? Today, C. G. Jung's most celebrated discovery is considered to be his empirical proof of the existence of a collective soul which he called the collective unconscious. Beginning in his own childhood, Jung noticed that some impressive dream and fantasy images could not be explained by *personal* experience. Later, within the framework of his duties as a doctor, he found that patients and analysands also spoke of such images, for which there were remarkable parallels in the history of religion.

---

[53] Ibid., §§ 713–14.
[54] Ibid.
[55] Ibid., § 715.

From this, Jung drew the conclusion that along with the personal unconscious which represents a layer of the psyche where experienced, forgotten and repressed contents are stored, there also exists a collective unconscious which has a general human, inherited psychic structure. One can imagine it to be a kind of field, an electromagnetic energy field, which, under the right conditions, can be made visible. Together with consciousness, it forms an unconscious-conscious whole, which is the foundation for all psychic processes.[56]

It is in the collective unconscious that the relatively independent centers, which Jung called the archetypes, are to be found. These are abstract dispositions, structural predispositions, or basic psychological patterns, which, in experience, appear as those basic elements which create specific ideas in the form of images. These are called archetypal images. Images, fantasies, or ideas can all be manifestations of archetypes which are shared by whole nations or eras. Archetypes can also be called "basic behavioral patterns" of the psyche, which can only be perceived as an inner psychical dynamic. Archetypes are an unconscious mechanism which can produce conscious collective ideas or images such as those we come across in myths, fairy tales, and legends.

Every archetype seems to be mysteriously linked to a corresponding instinct. They are like two poles at either end of a scale: at the spiritual end, inner psychical images appear which are laden with strong emotions; at the physical end, an individual would be overtaken by a strong instinct that drives him to perform some unreflected action. Usually, one fluctuates between these two extremes. However, it also varies from person to person and from one situation to another as to which pole is more activated. It is also part of the developmental process of an individual to become responsive to the stimulus of both poles simultaneously.[57]

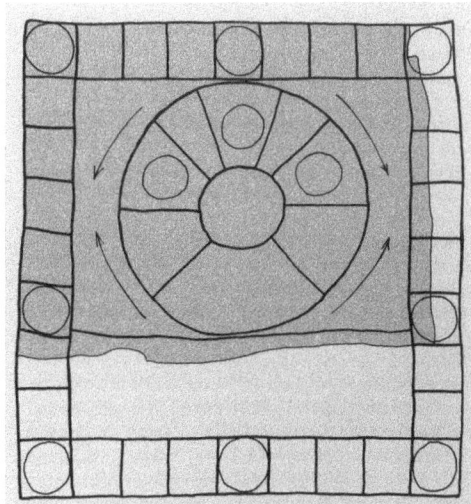

---

[56] Von Franz, *C. G. Jung*, 124.
[57] Von Franz, *Creation Myths*, 45–46.

The fact that there are existing multifarious archetypes, points to the danger that the human psyche has a latent tendency to dissociate. Man's tendency to be ruled by various archetypes is evident in the collective unconscious, but its opposite is also present; that is, the tendency toward cohesion, behind which is the archetype of wholeness as represented in the image of the unifying Anthropos-Christ and in the symbol of the mandala.[58]

In late-medieval Gerona, the archetype of wholeness behind the Creation Tapestry produced a mandala which rearranged the essential Christian world view and refocused the beliefs of the community threatened by Islam upon the central teachings of the Christian faith. Thus, the innermost circle of the Tapestry with its representation of the Pantocrator corresponds to the object or goal of contemplation, to the all-organizing source of all that is visible and invisible, to all that is animate and inanimate, and to the world as it is and to the hereafter.

In accordance with the Eastern viewpoint, a mandala not only expresses a psychical orientation toward the center and essence of an individual, that is, toward the Self, but rather it also has an effect upon its creator and upon those who contemplate it. Ancient, magical powers are hidden within it, for its origins reach back to the "circle of protection" within a spell, the magic which we know of from countless popular folk customs. It is the clear function of the image to keep a magical moat around the center in order to ward off any outer distractions.[59]

The motif of the mandala has a long history in our culture. Along with the emergence of the natural sciences in Greece in the 6th and 7th centuries B.C., there arose both a new image of God and a new way of looking at the basic structure of reality, namely, the idea of all existence having a common basis, and this basis having a circular or spherical structure, together with an inner order subject to its own laws. But this ancient image was only able to emerge clearly through the work of Plato and later, Plotinus. They postulated that circular motion is the motion of the soul and the spirit, and it regulates everything. The cosmos itself is a perfect sphere and thus is a perfect image of the spherical organism of existence, the world of ideas. Plotinus further

---

[58] Von Franz, *C. G. Jung,* 154.
[59] Jung, *Alchemical Studies,* vol. 13, *CW,* § 36.

developed this idea and passed it on to the Christian era. He said that the center of all being is the One, the Light which radiates in all directions into infinity. This One is enveloped by the sphere of the world soul and by the visible cosmos further out. The center, however, is the spiritual sphere, which is the One, Wholeness, and God simultaneously. This God is simultaneously the All-Embracing One and dwells deep within its depth, in its center. It is upon this that the famous sentence, "God is a spiritual sphere (or circle), whose center is everywhere and whose periphery is nowhere"[60] is based.

While in antiquity the mandala was seen as representing the godhead itself, as well as the cosmos and world soul, it gradually came to be seen primarily as an analogous image of the divine, as well as a symbol of the individual soul, and finally, as a representation of an "ideal self" or an "absolute self," in contrast to the limited, empirical ego.[61] Every image is also an inner image, a psychical image of an outer reality. From its projection onto the cosmos, the image returns in stages to its source, that is, into the inner world of the individual. This is why the mandala of the Creation Tapestry is not a representation of medieval reality in the sense of a divine revelation, but rather it depicts an integral psychic image of man as he was at that time, an image, however, which was projected onto outer reality. In this way, we, too, are given an insight into the medieval concept of the divine and the cosmos. The idea that man harbors a divine spark, or a likeness of the divine, in the depths of his soul was of central importance to some medieval mystics. Augustine had already said in connection with this, "God is more internal than my innermost"[62] and "God dwells in the hearts of men."[63] And in answer to the question as to when the Kingdom of God would come, Jesus replied: "The Kingdom of God is within you." (Luke, NT 17, 21).

Generally speaking, the circle in the mandala represents a natural wholeness as well as the all-embracing aspect of the soul. The square, on the other hand, stands for the conscious realization of its content. It refers particularly to what is earthbound, to the material world, to the body and to the realization of events in the here and now.[64]

---

[60] Von Franz, *C. G. Jung*, 143, see fn 15.
[61] Ibid.
[62] Augustinus, *Aufstieg zu Gott*, 97. (Translated by Kappes)
[63] Ibid., 79. (Translated by Kappes)
[64] Jung et al., *Man and his Symbols*, 249.

In this sense, the circle of the Gerona mandala with its image of the Pantocrator at its center, surrounded by all of creation, signifies not only the serene center of the world, the profundity of all being, the Divine and the *unus mundus*, but is also an image of the soul, of one's psychic center or the all-encompassing wholeness of a person, what Jung called "the Self." It is from within this center that the impulse arises for the micro- and macrocosm to develop. This development of both the micro- and macrocosm is symbolically portrayed by the depiction of the months at the edge of the tapestry, which, when viewed as a whole, lend the tapestry its quadratic shape. The illustrated scenes depict the eternal rhythm of birth and death, both in the life of each individual, as well as in nature as a whole.

The alchemists understood the opus, that is, the individuation process, to be an analogy of the formation of the world, even as the opus was looked upon as being God's creation. The "anthropos" of the alchemists was regarded as being a microcosm, that is, as being an exact replica of the world in miniature. Those elements within man which found correspondence with the macrocosm and which drew comparison to the formation of the world were seen to represent the birth of the Self, that is, the birth of the whole person who, in turn, was seen to be a microcosm.

Similar thoughts are expressed in a song by Anno, Archbishop of Cologne, who was an outstanding political and spiritual personality of the 11th century:

"Then he made a mixture of the two, this wise creator: human nature. It is a mix of both, body and soul. This is why it resembles the angels so closely. All that has been created in man."[65]

Here we find a description of unity between man and the universe. All of creation is to be found in man, that is, the microcosm is an exact replica of the macrocosm. This view was crucial to the medieval view of life, and through the insights of Jungian psychology, it has become relevant once again in a new form. The theory

---

[65] Annolied, II, 19–35 from Legner, *Monumenta Annonis*, 77. "At the beginning of the world, when there was nothing other than the word of creation and the shining of the light, when the holy hand of God brought into existence the many wondrous creations, He divided it all into two: one part he made into the physical world of the body, the other into the world of the spirit; *then he made a mixture of the two, this wise creator: human nature. It is a mix of both, body and soul. This is why it resembles the angels so closely. All that has been created in man,* accords with what is written in the Gospels. We should be seen as the third world, as the Greeks suggested several times over. This was the honor that was bestowed upon Adam, if only he had retained it!" (Translated by Kappes)

of the micro- and macrocosm was an integral part of medieval teachings from the time of the Carolingians forward, and the manuscripts from 9th to 12th centuries found in monastery and cathedral scholastic libraries are proof of this fact.[66]

Hildegard von Bingen[67] exclaims: "Oh man, do look at man more carefully: man already contains heaven and earth and all other creatures and nevertheless is a whole being [and] in him everything [creation] exists in concealed form." And elsewhere: "In that way God conceived [laid the seed for] all of creation in man."[68]

Thus, it can be said that the Creation Tapestry represents both the inner and the outer world, that is, it is an image of the totality of man and it is an image of the cosmos at large: the microcosm and the macrocosm.

It shows both man in his entirety, as well as the world at large, as emanating from God. It is not the "external" or "empirical" man who finds correspondence to the world at large, but rather, it is the totality of man, because this totality includes not only man's consciousness, but also the indeterminable dimension of the unconscious. The use of the term microcosm is, in itself, proof that there existed at the time a general notion that the "total man," the Anthropos, was as large as the whole world.[69]

As Geothe himself has pointed out: "Nothing's outside that's not within."[70]

And as Ibn 'Arabi has succinctly put it: "In contemplating Him, we contemplate ourselves, and in contemplating ourselves, He contemplates Himself."[71]

Whenever man is confronted by a last great unknown of fundamental importance, an image in the form of a mandala will be constellated both within, in one's soul, as well as externally, for the mandala is a symbol of a fundamental, transpersonal and meaningful order. This fact has also been proved by von Franz in the field of natural science with reference to modern models of the atom and to the latest theories on the structure

---

[66] Ibid., 90.
[67] Hildegard of Bingen (1098–1179), the great German mystic and visionary.
[68] Hildegard of Bingen, *Hildegard von Bingen,* 111. (Translated by Kappes)
[69] Jung, *Archetypes,* vol. 9/I, *CW,* § 550.
[70] Goethe, "Epirrhema," in *Poems and Epigrams,* 71.
[71] Ibn al 'Arabi, *Wisdom of the Prophets.*

of matter, the quantum.[72] When one looks at such a mandala, one sees beyond the multiplicity of the outer world and sees instead the images of a deeper reality which one carries within oneself.[73]

This double nature of a mandala representing both the inner and outer reality makes it possible for its center to represent both the divine as well as the Self. By arriving at this center, one reaches the "innermost man"; one meets "the noblest, god-like, innermost hidden man," who is made out of the "purest soul-substance."[74] This is the Kingdom of God, "where God lives and acts." [75] This explains the numinous effect which the Tapestry has upon people *for we see in the Tapestry not only an image of the cosmos and a new image of God, but also a reflection of our own all-embracing totality, the Self.*[76]

This concept largely corresponds to the inner truth about God and mankind as described by the Islamic Sufis. In their view, any attempt to formulate the Divine in concrete terms limits the illimitable. Therefore, believers are forbidden to make a concrete image of God as, in His infinite multiplicity, He remains unfathomable to human understanding. His essence, however, can find expression in an *abstract mandala,* whether it be in the form of a painting or in calligraphy, in a piece of woven fabric or *tapestry* or in an architectural structure. Such a symbolic representation of the Divine in mandala form always contains more than human understanding can perceive. In essence, it gives expression to the unity of divine being—the common denominator of the multiplicity of forms, the unity of plurality, so to speak. These thoughts have been summarized in one of the two articles of faith used when declaring oneself a Muslim: "There is no god, but Allah."[77] The realization of this thought puts an end to multiplicity and what remains is an integrated whole.

The second article of faith for a Muslim is: Muhammed is the Prophet of God. Contained within this thought is the concept of Mohammed as a "perfect human being," as a "universal prototype," an Anthropos or man

---

[72] Von Franz, *C. G. Jung,* 150ff.

[73] Ibid., 150.

[74] Ibid., 144, see fn 21–23.

[75] Ibid.

[76] On a fragment of papyrus, the following sentence by Oxyrhynchus has been handed down: "The Kingdom of Heaven is within you; and whoever shall know himself shall find it." Grenfell and Hunt, *New sayings of Jesus,* 15.

[77] Schimmel, *Träume des Kalifen,* 146. (Translated by Kappes)

in his totality, a microcosm which has its equivalent in the macrocosm.[78] Mohammed represents the union of all individual forms and meanings to be found in the universe.[79] All human potential is manifested in Him.[80] As Ibn 'Arabi puts it: "The Universal Prototype stands in the same relation to God as the pupil which is the instrument of vision to the eye. Through the Universal Prototype, God becomes conscious of Self in all the Divine aspects. The Universal Prototype is the eye of the world, whereby the Absolute sees Its own work."[81]

In Islam, a mandala is an abstract image of multiplicity contained within an integrated whole *and* of an integrated whole contained within a multiplicity; in other words, it is an abstract image of the divinity as well as of Mohammed, who represents man in his totality. A mandala is a depiction of the macrocosm and the microcosm: "The world has become a man, and man a world: There is no clearer explanation than this," writes Mahmud Schabistari.[82] Thus, both the Creation Tapestry and the Islamic mandala are based upon the same concept. But whereas the Christian mandala expresses a concrete image of the Divine, the Arabic image of God remains abstract. Both, however, share the structure of a mandala, as well as the idea of capturing in a single image "man in his totality" and the divine, as perceived from within and without. Bakhtiar expresses these Sufic thoughts as follows: "The mandala, as a reflection of the cosmos and cosmic processes within all things, works through numbers and geometry, beginning with Unity, moving through its theophany and back to Unity. It recapitulates at one and the same time, the permanence of paradise as an idea and its impermanence as a temporal reality. To the mystic it evokes the surrender to Self and the reintegration of the many into the One."[83]

---

[78] Bakhtiar, *Sufi*.
[79] Ibid., 10.
[80] Ibid., 11.
[81] Ibid.
[82] Ibid., 15.
[83] Ibid., 87.

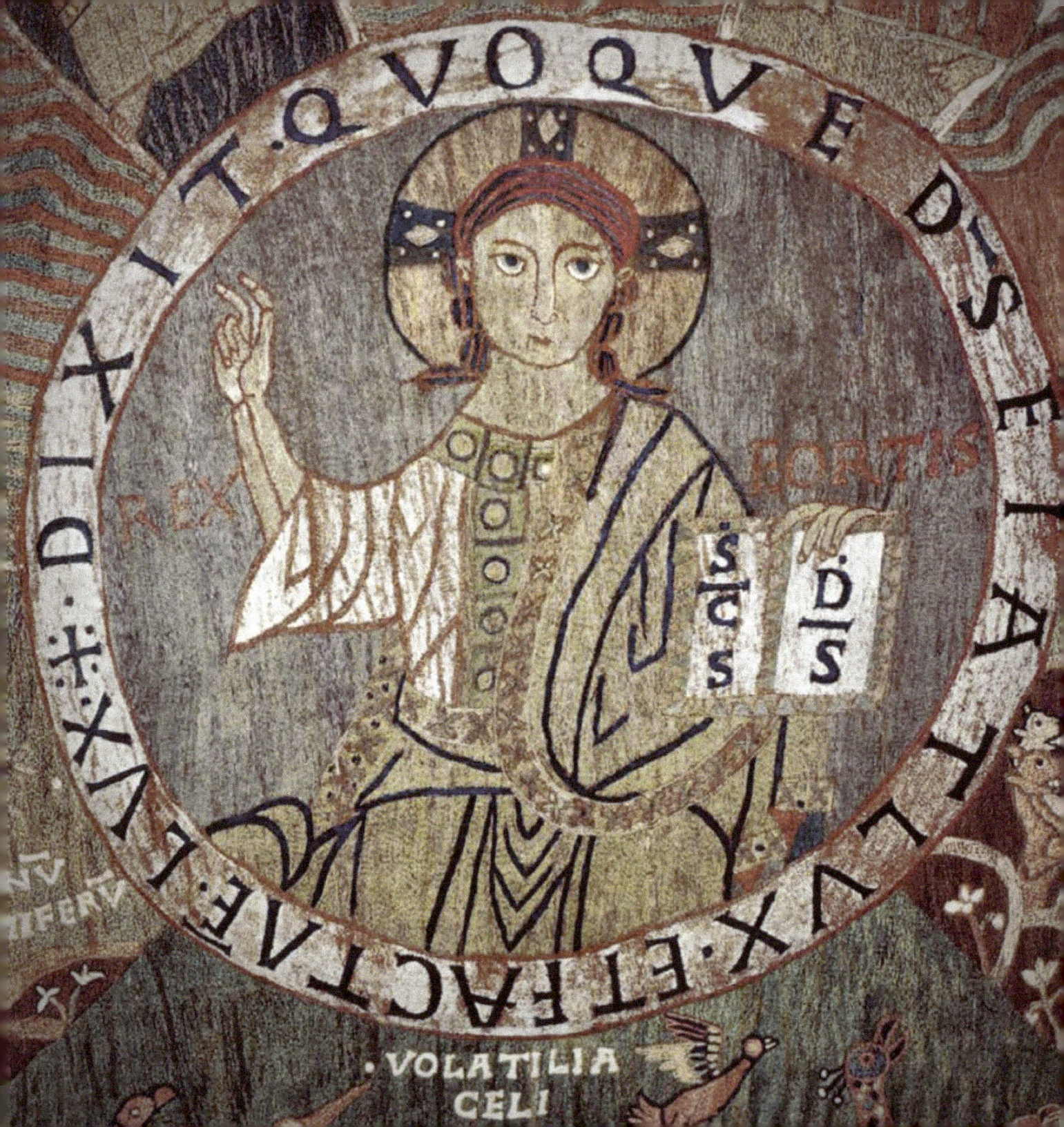

PRIMORDIAL BEGINNINGS – THE MALE AND FEMALE ASPECTS OF GOD

Medieval mystics imagined the divine foundation of the soul of man as being purely spiritual, a reflection of their Christian God. Thus, it excludes the natural world of creatures and of matter.

In this respect, there is a significant difference between the Creation Tapestry of Gerona as a medieval mandala and the concept of a personalized, masculine God-image. Namely, a mandala incorporates more feminine characteristics which find expression, for example, in Asia with Buddha sitting in the lotus position, or in the image of a Golden City. In the Western hemisphere, an example is the Garden of Eden divided into four parts (the four rivers of paradise, one depicted in each corner of the Creation Tapestry, are an illustration of this), and by representations of the Temenos (a sacred area), of a castle, of a round vessel, of heavenly Jerusalem. All these images share an essentially feminine symbolic nature. Thus, generally speaking, a mandala expresses an image of the divine which is closely related to Mother Earth and to the mother image of the material world.[84]

Through the fusion of the two patriarchal cultures of medieval Europe, that is, the Romanic and the Germanic, emerged a male-dominated Weltanschauung in the Western hemisphere, out of which arose a purely masculine personification of the Christian God-image, that is, God the Father. Early medieval man felt this one-sidedness and tried to integrate the female aspect of the divine into the world of the male logos, the same world to which our Western culture is still bound.

---

[84] Von Franz, *C. G. Jung*, 145.

At that time, however, this integration could only be attempted in the seclusion of a hermit's life for it went against the spirit of the time. Dramatic illustration of this point can be seen in the legend of St. Meinrad of the Dark Woods, now Einsiedeln (Switzerland).[85] It can also be recognized in the legend of the colonisation of the holy mountain of Catalonia, Montserrat (near Barcelona, Spain) by hermits who were said to have found a statue of a Black Madonna in a cave there. The focal point of their worship revolved around this statue of a *Black* Madonna who represents an earthy, more comprehensive image of Mary, whose influence has continued uninterrupted for over a thousand years and continues right up to the present time.

Since the Middle Ages, the relatively few places of pilgrimage with shrines to a Black Madonna are, nevertheless, among the most famous in Europe. They include Montserrat (Spain), Einsiedeln (Switzerland), Loreto (Italy), Czestochowa (Poland) and Altötting (Germany). Quispel even maintains that these dark images of Mary are the only living religious symbols in Europe today.[86]

Continuing this train of thought, it is an interesting fact that the Mother of God held a central position as protectress of the Romanesque cathedral of Gerona. In the cathedral museum, it is possible to view the statue of this Romanesque Madonna, measuring about 50 centimetres in length, with her boy-child sitting in her lap. She is carved out of olive-wood and was probably used to adorn the Romanesque altar of the cathedral. As the statue dates from the 12th century, she came into being at around the same time as the Romanesque buildings and, indeed, as the Creation Tapestry. At that time, the problem of integrating the feminine into the world of masculine logos was especially constellated as can be seen, for example, in the emerging tradition of the troubadours, as well as in the newly-arisen worship of Mary, but also in the countless witch hunts which soon followed as a counter-reaction to such pursuits.

From early on, there arose a compensatory movement to the masculine image of God in Judaism, firstly in the personification of "Wisdom" (Sophia) in the Book of Proverbs, one of the poetic books of the Old Testament. Here we find written (8:22–31):

> "The Lord possessed me at the beginning of His

---

[85] Etter, *Meinrad*; and Etter, "Einsiedler Meinrad."
[86] Quispel, "Schwarze Madonna."

way, before His works of old

I was set up from everlasting from the beginning, or

ever the earth was.

When He appointed the foundations of the earth:

then I was by Him, as one brought up with Him, and I

was daily His delight, rejoicing always before Him."

This personification of Wisdom is a female goddess of the metropolis, a mother-mistress, like the Babylonian Ishtar. Her representation as a tree brings to mind the numerous other Semitic love, and mother, goddesses. In one of the Books of the Apocrypha, The Wisdom of Solomon, there is a female figure depicted as a world-creating Pneuma. She is friendly toward humans, and is a judicious and holy spirit who is a constant companion of God Himself and mirrors His eternal light within all things. At the time of early gnosis, the Holy Ghost, who appeared as a dove, was thought of as being Sophia, Sapienta or Wisdom, as well as the Mother of Christ.[87]

It is written in Genesis that, in the beginning, the Spirit of God hovered over the elemental waters. In the Creation Tapestry, this Spirit is represented as a dove. This is, then, the feminine side of the One, the divine Wisdom (Sapienta Dei), divine omniscience, the feminine spiritual aspect of the male logos God. She is the soul of the world, the anima mundi.

The waters in the Creation Tapestry correspond to the pre-celestial, primordial waters which contain all divine creative power. From an early date, these waters were interpreted as being a symbol for the Holy Ghost in patristic literature. The four rivers of paradise have their source in these same waters.[88]

The translation of the word "to hover" in Hebrew is a derivative of a root word which can also mean "to weave" or "to brood." Thus, the first text addresses typically feminine activities.[89] In this way, the very fact

---

[87] Jung, *Psychology and Religion*, vol. 11, *CW*, §§ 609ff; and von Franz, *C. G. Jung*, 148–49.
[88] Von Franz, *Passion of Perpetua*, 37.
[89] I am indebted to Ms. E. Hoerni-Jung for this information, for which I give her my warm thanks.

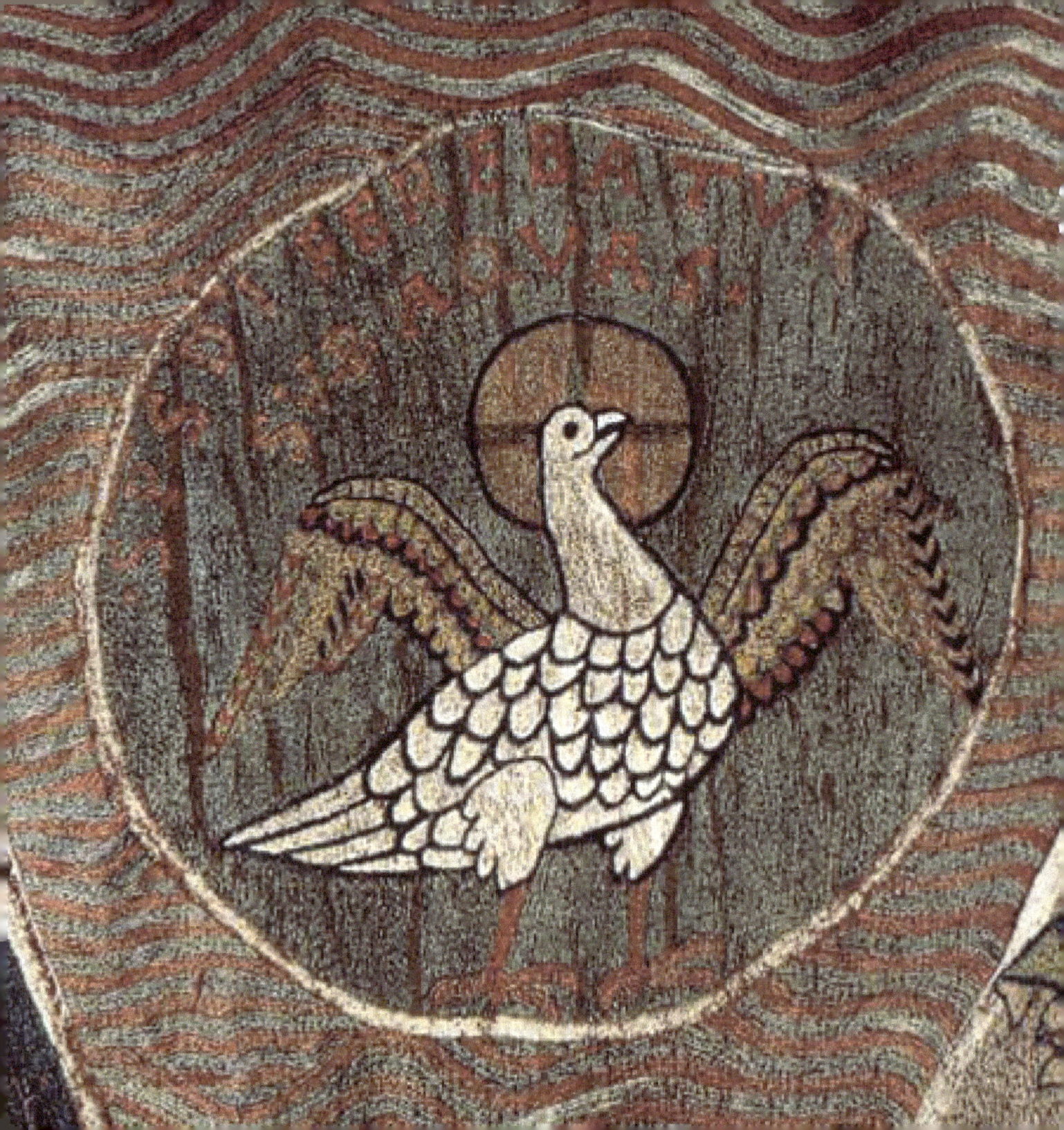

that the mandala of the Creation Tapestry is a work of embroidery rather than being a painted image underlines its wholly feminine aspect.

The Gospel according to St. John begins with the following words:

> "In the beginning was the Word, and the Word
> was with God, and the Word was God.
> The same was in the beginning with God.
> All things were made by Him; and without Him
> was not any thing made that was made.
> In Him was life; and the life was the light of men.
> And the light shineth in darkness;
> and the darkness comprehended it not."[90]

The Christian God-image in the form of the dove in the Creation Tapestry of the Romanesque Church of Mary in Gerona is represented as having a feminine nature; the dove represents the creative power of the feminine through whose emanation the world was created. Our attention is already drawn to this feminine-masculine double aspect of God in the introduction to Adam's family tree in Genesis (5:1):

> "When God created Adam, He made him in God's
> image; as man and woman He made them.
> And He blessed them and gave them the name
> 'Adam' (that is, man), when He created them."

With its colored wings and its halo, the white dove which hovers over the primordial waters in the middle-segment above the Pantocrator symbolizes the feminine aspect of the divine as revealed in His omniscience and in His creative powers. And as an inner image, the dove is a symbol of the maternal foundation of the soul. In Islam, the soul is of divine origin and corresponds to the human psychic structure. The soul in Islam represents the principle of the feminine.

---

[90] John 1:1–5.

In Sufism, God is assigned a dual role: a passive one as the receiver of ideas, and an active one as the creator of all that is to be born. Thus, Allah has both feminine as well as masculine qualities. In addition, Islam has named two important aspects of the divine which are connected to the feminine function of creation, that is, "*Khalq* und *Bari.*" Khalq refers to that aspect of creation which conceives of the potential in all things. This is also known as eternal wisdom or Sophia. Sufis see this divine function symbolised in the Virgin Mary for she was the receptacle of the Holy Ghost. Further, the Virgin Mary is also a symbol of the second divine feminine aspect, "Bari," which denotes that which brings forth the Holy Ghost.[91] Both these aspects, active and passive, are part of the very essence of the Creator.[92] FATIMA, the daughter of the Prophet, is called "the creative feminine" by the Sufis. "It is the concept of the Creative Feminine which holds the secret of Lordship."[93] FATIMA symbolizes the essence of the feminine because she is the creator of the Holy Ghost which in turn created her.[94]

It is remarkable that both the worship of, and appreciation for, FATIMA in Islam today is increasingly noticeable and, simultaneously, that the role of the Mother of God, Mary, in Catholic Christianity is also undergoing revalorization.

Sufism sees an inner dualism in both men and women; irrespective of one's sex, both masculine and feminine principles are at work in both, and further, both men and women have within them an action-oriented, doing aspect as well as a passive, receiving aspect. These attributes are complementary and are essentially of equal value. There is no masculine aspect without its feminine equivalent, no active principle without its passive (hidden or apparent) equivalent. Both attributes find completion in their opposite.[95]

Irrespective of race or cultural heritage, nearly every creation myth contains the motif of splitting apart to signify the beginning of creation. In Babylonian culture, Marduk splits apart the original parent-couple or the primal monster, Tiamat, into heaven and earth. Very often one finds the image of an original egg or

---

[91] Bakhtiar, *Sufi*, 82.
[92] Ibid., 21.
[93] Ibid., 82.
[94] Ibid.
[95] Ibid., 102.

source of light at the beginning of creation. Cosmogonical events begin with the division or splitting apart of this one thing. In India, the sun emerges from an egg contained within the primal waters. In a cosmogonical image from ancient Egypt, the moment of creation is depicted by the formation of a large egg out of which the sun god, Ra, emerges. In Orphism, an egg is formed in primeval space and out of it comes Phanes, Erikapaios, and Metis. Out of one half of the egg, the heavens are fashioned; out of the other half, the earth. Essentially the same images are to be found amongst the Oceanic peoples and the Native Americans. The myth of the cosmogonic egg and its division is also to be found in both China and Persia, as well as in India.[96]

If we look at creation from the opposite direction, that is, from the angle of its origins, then the moment of creation can be viewed as a disturbance of the primeval order of things, as a weakening of the original world of the gods as symbolized by their descent into the here and now. Thus, begins a pattern that sets up a tension, which, in turn, underlies the dynamics of existence. In the opening verse of the Kalevala, a Finnish creation myth, the world is created by the destruction of the seven primeval eggs upon the knee of a hermaphroditic primeval being. Here, too, a bird, either a duck or an eagle, which represents the creative, feminine spirit of the divine, is the bringer of the primeval eggs.

In many creation myths it is the feminine which first splits off from the masculine; however, perhaps even more often, the masculine splits off from the feminine. Thus, an irreversible process of development is set into motion, a process which is forever moving onward. In an Iroquoian myth, one finds expression of this tragic disturbance of the original divine order of things, for it tells of the primordial fathers falling ill.[97]

This male-female double aspect of the divine is also reflected in the colors which were chosen for the Tapestry. In fact, the great impression which the Tapestry makes upon one is partly due to its warm colors, subtle shades of which vivify each individual picture. Over the years, the Tapestry has gradually become

---

[96] Von Franz, *Symbolism in Fairy Tales*, book in preparation: in the German version *Symbolik des Märchens*, book 2, vol. II (Küsnacht: Stiftung für Jung'sche Psychologie, 2018), 119–20.
[97] Von Franz, *Creation Myths*, 28ff.

more pastel in color because of the repeated interweaving of woollen threads of a slightly different shade at each restoration. Nevertheless, individual original colors are still clearly discernible.

Red and blue are the two main colors which make up the background of the Pantocrator, that is, the upper half of the inner circle (the segment with the dove, from the first to the fourth days of creation), along with the middle segment of the lower half of the inner circle (the fish of the sea and the birds of the air). The primordial waters are depicted by bands of wavy lines in blue and red. In the natural world, both the sky and the waters of the earth (including the ocean as the source of all living things) are blue. Viewed symbolically, the color blue represents all that is timeless and eternal as well as all that is boundless and infinite. To sky and water we associate inner calm, peace, serenity, wisdom, perhaps even a feeling of coming home, of communion with oneself, of introversion. Blue is also the color of smoke which rises up to the sky. Accordingly, blue has more feminine qualities and refers to the feminine spiritual aspect.[98] Indeed, this is why the Mother of God in Christian art often wears a dark blue heavenly cloak.[99] Faust prays to her in the following manner:

"Pavilioned in the heavens blue
Queen on high of all the world
for the holy sight I sue
of the mystery unfurled."[100]

The color red, by contrast, represents fire, its glowing embers, and also blood. It stands for warmth, for coming of age, for one's emotional life with its pleasures and its pain, for vitality, for motivation, action, and the drive to create. But red also incorporates the aspect of burning, of being consumed, of destruction, as well as of death and rebirth, of limitation and the temporal nature of life. The color red, then, refers to a masculine-materialistic aspect. Mars, the Roman god of war, is red and the planet of the same name, when

---

[98] The dark blue, patched dress was known in Islam to be "the badge of the aspirants of Sufism." It was worn as a visible sign of one having turned one's back on the world and it meant, on the one hand, sorrow and grief, and on the other, a turning toward the world of the spirit that is outside of time and space; cf. Schimmel, *Mystical Dimensions of Islam*, 102.
[99] Riedel, *Farben*, 48ff.
[100] Goethe, *Dramen: Faust*, vol. 4, *Goethes Werke*, 390. (Translated by Kappes)

viewed through a telescope, has a reddish hue. The astronomical symbol of Mars, "O," is the current symbol we use to denote masculinity per se. And finally, it is in March (Marcius meaning Mars) that spring begins, that is, it is the month in which nature begins its annual process of self-renewal.[101]

Red and blue are contrasting colors. They lie at either end of the visible spectrum of color; red preceding the longwave band of infra-red, and blue preceding the shortwave band of ultra-violet. Red and blue can thus be seen as a true pair of opposites. They are the first differentiation of the white, undifferentiated light (as represented in the white garment of the Pantocrator and the body of the dove) for they represent the visible extremes of the color spectrum. Red and blue are used alternately in the inner circle of the Creation Tapestry to depict the bands of wavy lines of the primordial waters and thereby emphasize the male/female aspect of both the primordial origins of creation and of the *unus mundus*. Blue is the dominant color of the small circles of the segments which depict the first and fourth days of creation. The contrast between the angel of light and the angel of darkness is highlighted by the color of their garments. Lux, the angel of light, is clothed in a red garment with a blue cloak, while Tenebris, the angel of darkness, wears a blue garment with a red cloak. When viewed as a whole, the red-blue coloring of the inner circle of creation emphasizes the male/female aspect of both the divine and the Self.

---

[101] Riedel, *Farben*, 16ff.

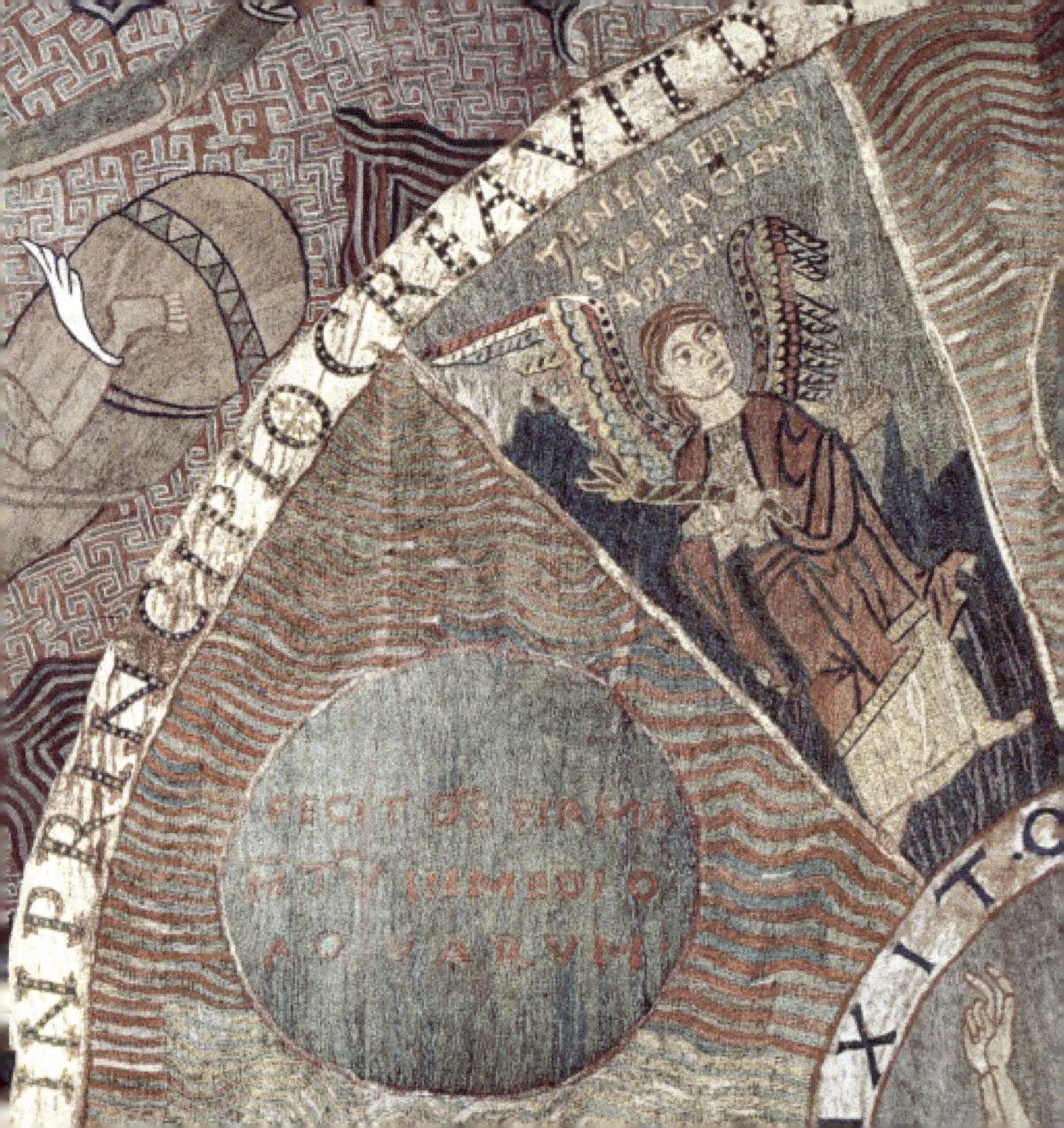

...N PRINCIPIO CREAVIT D...

TENEBRE ERAN
SVB FACIEN
ABISSI.

FECIT DS FIRMA
M... IIMMEDIO
A... ARVM

...XIT.O

THE FIRST FOUR DAYS OF CREATION

The images that together make up the inner circle of creation clearly refer to Genesis,[102] although they do not depict the narrative in a strict sense but rather in a more interpretative manner. Moreover, the timeless aspect of creation is accentuated by both the circular form divided as it is into eight segments, thereby forming a mandala, as well as by the absence of a strictly sequential order in the images depicted.

The first creation story can be summarized as follows:

On the first day God said: Let there be light. And there was light. On the second day God said: Let there be a firmament in the midst of the waters and let it divide the waters above and below. And God called the firmament heaven. On the third day God said: Let the waters under the heaven be gathered together in one place so that the dry land may become visible. And God called the dry land earth and the gathering together of the waters called the seas. And God also said: Let the earth bring forth grass, the herb yielding seed and the fruit yielding fruit after their kind, whose seed is in itself upon the earth.

On the fourth day God said: There shall be light in the firmament of the heavens to divide day from night and let them be indicators for the seasons, days and years, and let them be lights in the firmament of the heavens to give light upon the earth and rule day and night and divide light and darkness. On the fifth day God said: Let the water be filled with living creatures and birds shall fly above the earth in the firmament of the sky. On the sixth day God said: Let the earth bring forth living creatures: cattle, creeping things and beasts of the field, each after his kind. And God said: Let us make man in our image, after our likeness. And

---

[102] Gen. 1:1–31.

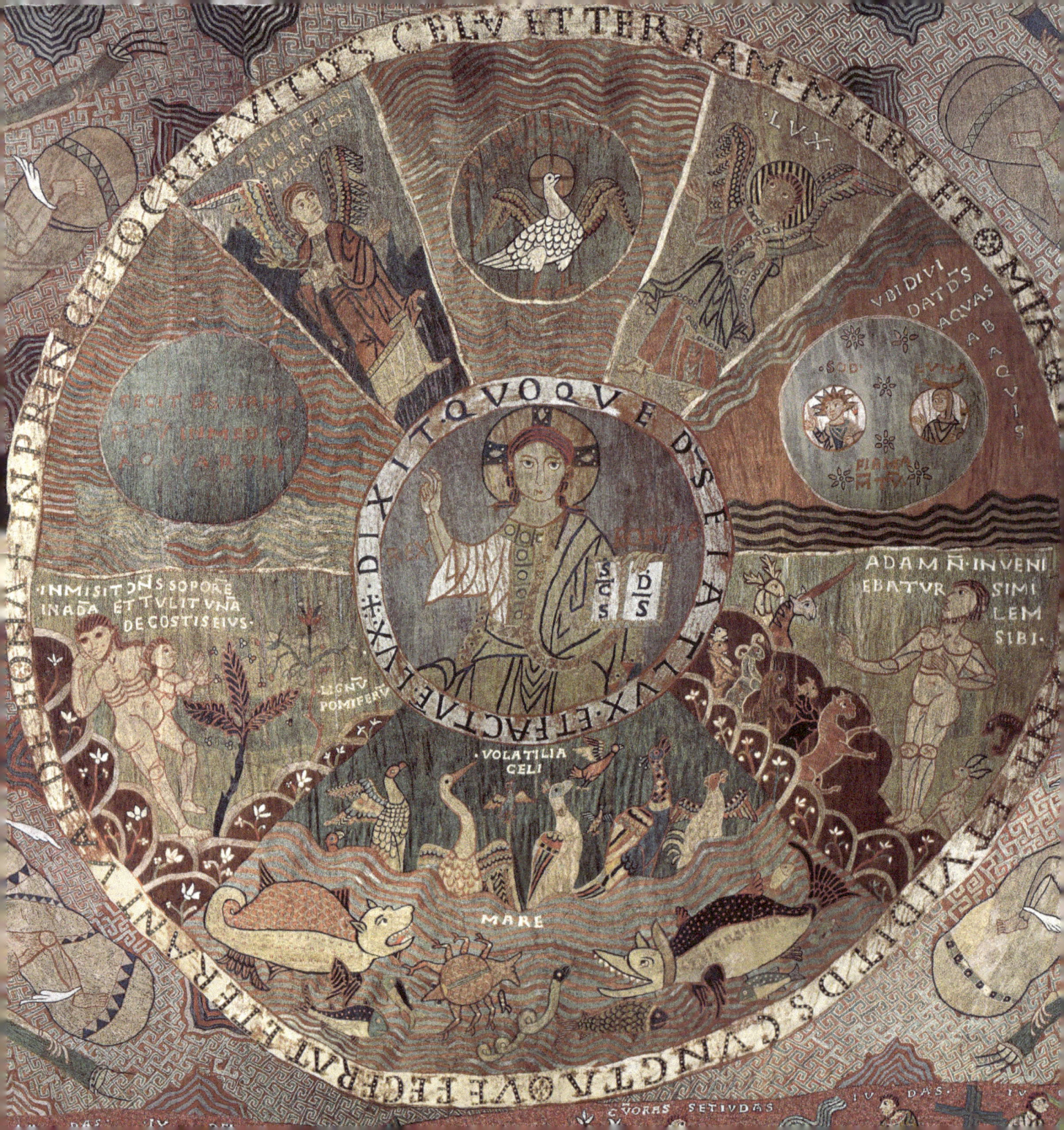

on the seventh day God ended his work which he had made: and he rested on the seventh day from all his work which he had made.

The second creation story is rather different from the first:[103]

And the Lord God formed man from the dust of the ground, breathed into his nostrils the breath of life; and man became a living soul. And the Lord God planted a garden eastward in Eden; and there he put the man whom he had formed. And out of the ground made the Lord God grow different trees that are pleasant to see and good for food, and the tree of knowledge of good and evil. A river went out of Eden to water the garden; from there it divided into four heads: Pison, Gihon, Tigris, and Euphrates. And the Lord God commanded the man and said: Of every tree in the garden you may freely eat: but of the tree of knowledge of good and evil, thou shalt not eat: in the day that you eatest thereof thou shalt surely die. And out of the ground the Lord God formed every beast of the field, and every fowl of the air; and brought them unto man to see what he would call them: And whatsoever man called every living creature, that was the name thereof. And Adam gave names to all cattle, and to the fowl of the air and to every beast of the field. And the Lord God caused a deep sleep to fall upon Adam, and he slept: and He took one of his ribs, and closed up the place with flesh. And the Lord God fashioned a woman from the rib he had taken from man and brought her unto man. She shall be called woman because she was taken out of man. And the two, man and woman, were naked and were not ashamed.

On the first day God created light: "And the Lord said let there be light and there was light." This text is written on a white band surrounding the Pantocrator. He separated light from darkness, the one only being able to come about because of the existence of the other. In this way, the double nature of the divine was manifested from the outset. The male/female aspects which together make up His totality have a light and a dark side. Since the first day of creation, this male/female god-image has existed. In the Old Testament, the light and the dark side of the divine find impressive unity in Jahweh. There is a legend which says that when God became man in Jesus, he saw how Satan simultaneously fell to earth. The light and the dark side of god became incarnate in Jesus, and in Satan or the Anti-Christ. This is why Jung calls Satan "the Shadow of

---

[103] Ibid., 2:5–25.

Christ."[104] This light and dark side of the divine find expression in the Creation Tapestry in the figures of the angel of light (LUX) and the angel of darkness (TENEBRIS) which can be found on either side of the dove.

Islam holds a more differentiated view of evil as personified by Satan or Iblis. In the Koran, evil is referred to either as a fallen angel or as a djinn who was born from fire, and who played an important role in the story of creation as the teacher of the angels. According to a well-known tradition, Satan was present from the beginning, in the blood of Adam's children and thus became equated with the inferior principle of "flesh" or matter. Man, however, always has the possibility to resist Satan who is never purely evil but is also a creature of God and as such is an indispensable tool in His hand (see page 72).[105]

The famous German prophetess, Hildegard von Bingen, who lived approximately at the time the Tapestry was being made, also commented on the story of creation in the following manner:

"And the word of the Father sounded: 'there shall be light!' – and all became light and the world was filled with radiant beings. For the word 'there shall be light' does not just describe the creation of any odd light, but that 'especially conceived light,' those beings made of light, which are angels. But when He said: 'There shall be light' it initially meant the substance of light which we see in front of us. But Lucifer saw in the North a free space, empty of creation: that was where he wanted to establish his own dominion of far richer and more magnificent creations than God's, for he knew nothing of the divine plan to create other creatures. He had not seen the countenance of the Father, nor did he know His omnipotence or had tasted of His benevolence; so, without knowledge of God he tried to put himself against God. That is how Good and Evil fell asunder: neither did Good meet Evil nor Evil Good. God stayed intact as perfect as a wheel. God is like a wheel, in the same way the wheel is a symbol for perfection."[106]

From the very beginning, everything has had both a light and a dark side. Every archetype contains both aspects, which is why its effect can be equally positive and constructive, as well as negative and destructive.

---

[104] Jung, *Psychology and Religion*, vol. 11, *CW*, §§ 248ff; Lammers, Cunningham and Stein, *Jung-White Letters*, 218.
[105] Schimmel, *Mystical Dimensions of Islam*, 193.
[106] Hildegard of Bingen, *Hildegard von Bingen*, 109–10. (Translated by Kappes)

The positive aspect of any archetype is behind all creative achievement; for example, in science, it is the force which brings about new ideas and basic concepts. The negative aspect of any archetype manifests itself in blind fanaticism, ideological narrow-mindedness and in manias. Both for an individual as well as for the collective, such negative aspects can become manifest in psychotic episodes. Indeed, archetypal contents can delude or, equally, they can have a culturally beneficial effect. All human endeavor can thus be seen as having both light and dark aspects. Today, we are confronted by this light/dark double aspect of human endeavor in a particularly painful way. For far too long, for almost 200 years, our collective belief in salvation through so-called "progress" has blinded us to its disastrous and destructive aspect. According to a Swiss legend, progress is only possible with the help of the devil who, in return, may lay claim to a human soul.[107] Such traditional knowledge has been completely forgotten for the last 200 years. As the industrial revolution gained momentum at the outset of the 19th century, it became so self-evident to the great majority of people that technology was both brilliant and advantageous that the few warnings which were issued were brushed aside as being signs of incorrigible pessimism or primitive backwardness. In certain circles today, there are still some who consider conservationists to be criminal red-green enemies of the state. It would seem that in our time, the dark aspect of technological progress is evident, surrounded as we are by its destructive, contaminating, poisonous, suffocating, health-endangering aspects, and it is here that the dark side of God is manifested.[108]

There is much talk about both the difficulty of addressing these issues along with the often depressing insight that no solution to our existential problems exists that could do justice to all sides. Hence, a fundamental fact, which has been given symbolic expression in the Creation Tapestry, needs to be made conscious, namely, that in all our decision-making, both aspects, the light and the dark, must be resolutely taken into consideration. This means that every day, each one of us is repeatedly faced with the moral task of becoming aware of both aspects of our actions, and their consequences, in everything we do, but that we must nevertheless go ahead and do whatever we feel called upon to do. This means, however, that we must learn

---

[107] Keckeis, "D'Tifelsbrugg und d'r Tifelsstei," 31.

[108] Recently, an elderly man dreamt of the raging destruction of the environment as being the Third World War that had already broken out.

to bear the tension of the opposites. We must take up our position between good and evil without yielding to either principle, no matter how great our suffering is. If, however, we do inwardly align ourselves with one of the principles, then the other sinks back into the unconscious, to reappear in outer reality as our own projection. When this happens, we once again adopt the erroneous view that we have finally been able to identify the seat of all evil with whom we must do battle, be it a member of the right or left wing, the economy, the military establishment, communism, car-drivers, our neighbors, one's husband or wife, and so on. This experience of being torn between the opposites is depicted in Christianity by the image of Jesus being crucified on the cross. Generally, the symbol of the cross often represents this problem on both an individual and collective level. Both the discovery of the cross, as well as the suffering this discovery engenders by bringing this problem into conscious awareness, are the subject of the legend of the Finding of the Cross by St. Helena, which is portrayed in the lower fragmented part of the Tapestry (see below page).

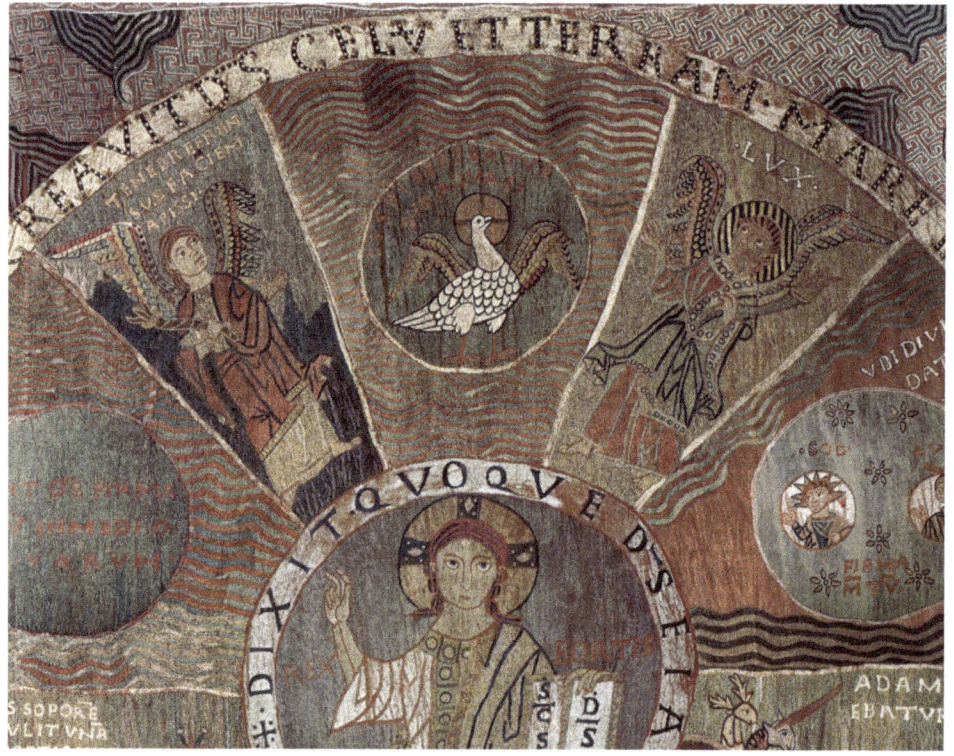

In nature, too, a dark, destructive principle vies with a light, constructive one. On the one hand, the whole of nature is constantly under threat of extinction, for example, through natural catastrophes such as forest or steppe-land fires, volcanic eruptions, famine, and epidemics. In addition, there is also the threat of global climatic changes, changes of sea level, as well as changes in the composition of the air. Further, with increasing entropy, nature is moving ever-closer to a so-called thermal death. On the other hand, over millions of years, animate nature has been developing an increasingly complex creative order throughout the whole of the biosphere. This is what we call "evolution," by which we mean a higher development from earlier forms, an orthogenesis, with human consciousness representing its present culmination.

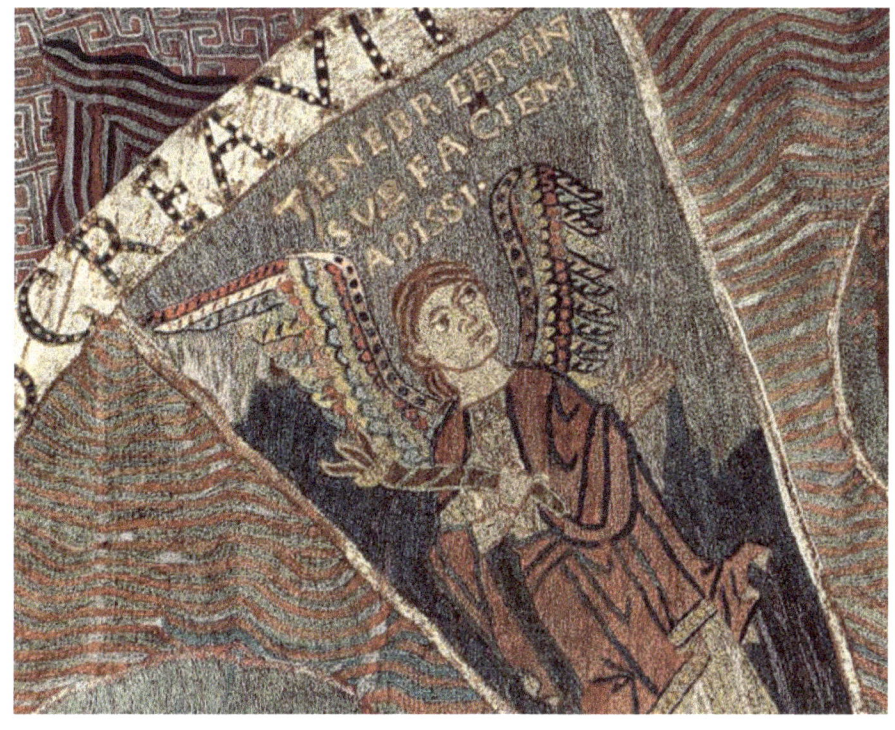

Let us return to the Creation Tapestry. This male/female, light/dark quaternity corresponds to the totality at the origin of all creation, to the divine chaos or the divine primordial order. At the beginning was Chaos or Tohuwabohu.[109] We are, therefore, talking about an all-encompassing, primordial basis for all existence out of which, alone, all further development could come about and become increasingly differentiated. The Hebrew expression for the origin of all creation is "Barbke Eloha," which means "in four is God" and represents the totality of the divine primordial basis of all creation.[110] I would like to call this original condition with its quaternal totality the inner layer or the *protoarchetype of the psyche.*

---

[109] Tohu wahohu (Hebrew) means formless and formed; Khaos (Greek) means void, disorder, gap. Scholem, *Geheimnisse der Schöpfung*, 55ff.

[110] Ibid., 49ff.

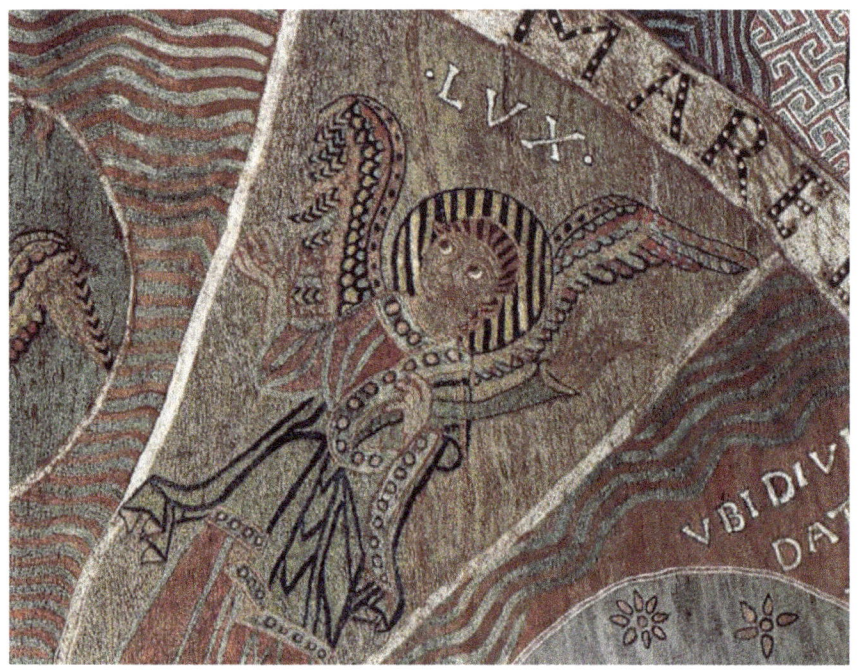

In "Liber Divinorum Operum," Hildegard of Bingen calls this basic precondition "basic material" or "primordial material." It is the basis out of which all earthly and celestial beings come into existence and it underlies all earthly and celestial creation. Given by God before time began, this "primordial material" underlies all creatures of both heaven and earth. Thus, it is the basic pattern behind all of reality and the potential of every creature and of all matter to exist and finds eternal containment within it.[111] In this way, Hildegard's idea of a "primordial material" corresponds to Jung's idea of an archetype, and to what I have called the "protoarchetype," with the sole intention of making a linguistic distinction between the "primordial matter" of life and all other archetypes.

Every religion needs an idiom of its own in order to elucidate God's manifestations in outer reality. "In Sufism, the language of expression is that of the Archetypes or Divine Names and Qualities."[112] Bakhtiar continues: "The Godhead in Its unmanifest quality is above every quality we could ascribe to It. This is the Divine Essence about which one can say nothing, for any description would only serve to limit or bind It. Divine Essence manifests Itself, however, in the direction of Creation through stages, the first of which is

---

[111] Hildegard of Bingen, *Hildegard von Bingen*, 66ff.
[112] Bakhtiar, *Sufi*, 13.

the Archetypes, the possibilities contained within the Absolute."[113] "These archetypes, which are also referred to as divine names and attributes, are the potential contained within the absolute. They are between the absolute and the perceived world."[114] Sufis are able to perceive the names of God or the archetypes as a symbol of inner potential, as well as recognizing them in outer reality. The creative

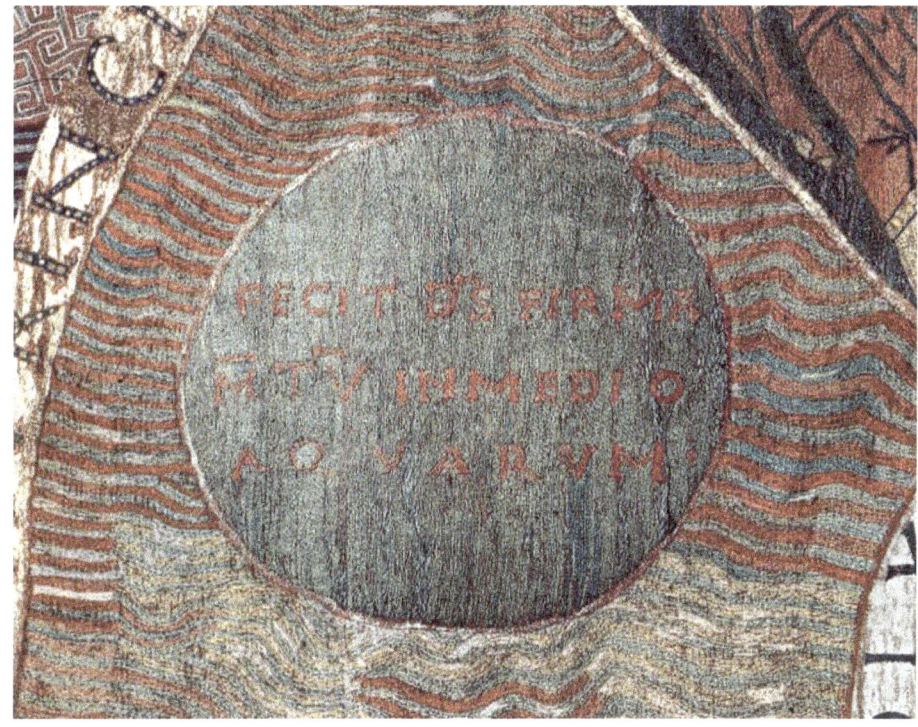

task of an artist is simply to be inwardly ready to give an outer, recognizable form to a carpet, for example, in a manner which reveals his own inner spiritual potential. Ibn 'Arabi defines the names of God as "Universal Ideas" or "universals," and he goes on to say "that the Universal Ideas (*al-umur al-kulliyah*), which evidently have no individual existence as such, are nonetheless present, intelligibly and distinctly, in the mental state; they always remain interior with respect to individual existence, yet determine everything that pertains to this."[115] Further, he writes: "although the Divine Names may be infinite as to their multitude— for one knows them by that which flows from them and which is equally unlimited—they are nonetheless reducible to a definite number of 'roots' which are the 'mothers' of the Divine Names or the (Divine)

---

[113] Ibid.
[114] Ibid.
[115] Ibn al 'Arabi, *Wisdom of the Prophets*, 13–14.

Presences integrating the Name."[116] These "mothers" of the names of God correspond to what I call here the protoarchetypes.

Ibn 'Arabi understands the Godhead to be the "Being beyond all being." It is beyond space and time. It has absolute existence and eternal reality. In this manner, he links the idea of a continual divine emanation with a perpetual act of divine creation. The divine is symbolised by the limitless sea in which the universal Self is absorbed like a drop of water, or it is symbolised by water out of which, once it is frozen, the world is crystallised.[117]

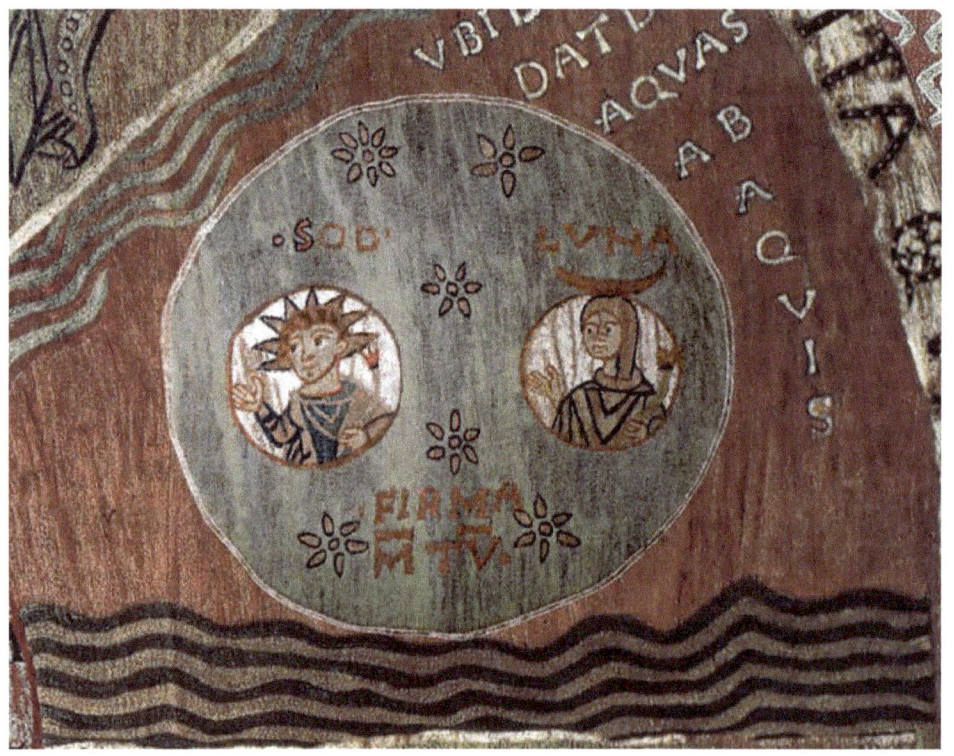

"Darkness and light are the archetypical symbols of Sufism because they are natural, immediate self-expressions of a root experience of the Divinity. They denote the stations of annihilation (fanā') and subsistence (baqā'). These stations are metaphysical experiences which occur only at a transcendental level of awareness."[118] If there is no conscious perception of an object or the ego, then one is

---

[116] Ibid., 28.
[117] Schimmel, *Mystical Dimensions of Islam*, 5.
[118] Bakhtiar, *Sufi*, 90.

moving toward the dark. Darkness is submergence in the unconscious. To step into the light corresponds to enlightenment, to being awakened to the world in which the divine essence itself is manifested. In this manner, the mystic is in touch with his inner images which help him become aware of the divine core at the center of his being. For Sufis, light and dark are inner experiences that find repeated symbolic expression in numerous art forms.

Primeval existence is without form, yet it has form. The primal waters represent a place of no determination or form, but it is not real and has no existence. In the same way, primal light is not perceivable but is the hidden primal light. This is how the mysteries of creation, the fundamental condition of primeval existence, are described in the cabbalistic chapter in the Book of Sohar.[119]

Out of this primeval beginning, *a new day dawned, the second day*, when God divided the waters and created in their midst a firmament, the heavens. On *the third day* of creation, according to Genesis, God gathered the waters into one place, whereupon dry land—the earth—appeared. In the Creation Tapestry, the creation of earth under the sky on the third day of creation is not specifically portrayed. There is no doubt, however, that this deed is shown as being a part of the image for *the fourth day*, when time was created. The origin of plants is also mentioned in Genesis as having taken place on the third day, but is postponed to a later day in the Creation Tapestry. The plant world appears in the Creation Tapestry for the first time on *the fifth day*, the same day in which Adam and the animals of the world appear. This reversal of the order of creation in the Tapestry makes sense, because the sun, as the giver of life, is thus created before the plant world, instead of the other way around. In addition, such a postponement means that the creation of plants, animals and man is united in one act of creation involving all forms of life.

Out of the primal quaternio of the Existing One, little by little, there begins a process of differentiation by means of division, but not within the framework of time, for time has yet to be created. In the middle of the primal waters (the protoarchetype of the psyche), the firmament or heavens comes into being. On *the third day* under this firmament, the primal waters collect in one place, thereby revealing that which is dry, the earth or "materie." During this phase of creation which takes place outside of time, we are again confronted

---

[119] Scholem, *Geheimnisse der Schöpfung.*

with the image of the division of primal matter into four aspects, which together are the precondition for life. This division takes place in four stages and is concluded on *the fourth day*, with the creation of the "sun," "moon," and "stars," when day becomes separated from night. In this way, the precondition for space, matter, and time are created.

With the division of the primal waters and the formation of heaven, "space" comes into being on the *second day*, which is *the protoarchetype of space*. With the collection of the primal waters in one place, "land" appears on the *third day*, which is *the protoarchetype of matter* or Materie. Through the creation of the "sun," "moon," and "stars" on the *fourth day*, the rhythm of day and night is created along with the cycle of the moon, the seasons of the year and the preformation of the year itself, that is, *the protoarchetype of time* has come into existence.

I call these the protoarchetypes because all of them came into existence through division, thereby increasing the gradient and the tension and are effectively the precondition for everything that follows. *Within the confines of this quaternio—of psyche, space, matter, and time—that is, within their primal presupposition, all empirical reality exists*. It takes place within this four-dimensional space or field of tension. The fifth, the *quinta essentia*, is life or the protoarchetype of life, and it arises out of the pre-existing quaternio. *Life in all its forms takes place within this field of space and time, of psyche and matter*. I call this the second layer or protoarchetype of life, again symbolised by a quaternio. By using the word "protoarchetypes" I mean simply the basic archetypal experiences of humanity.

During the first four days, God did nothing but divide: light from darkness or the primal waters. He differentiated. The beginning of life signifies the first real act of creation, for only then did God create something completely new. Being the fifth protoarchetype, life is at the center of the differentiated quaternio of pre-existing protoarcheypes and is the factor which connects them all into one unified whole. This is represented in the Creation Tapestry in *one* picture in the lower half of the circle, and this single picture is divided into three segments: the middle segment depicts the creation of the creatures of the sea and of the air; the segment on the right depicts the creation of plants and the animals of the field and woods, as well as the creation of Adam himself; the segment on the left depicts the appearance of Eve out of Adam's rib. This

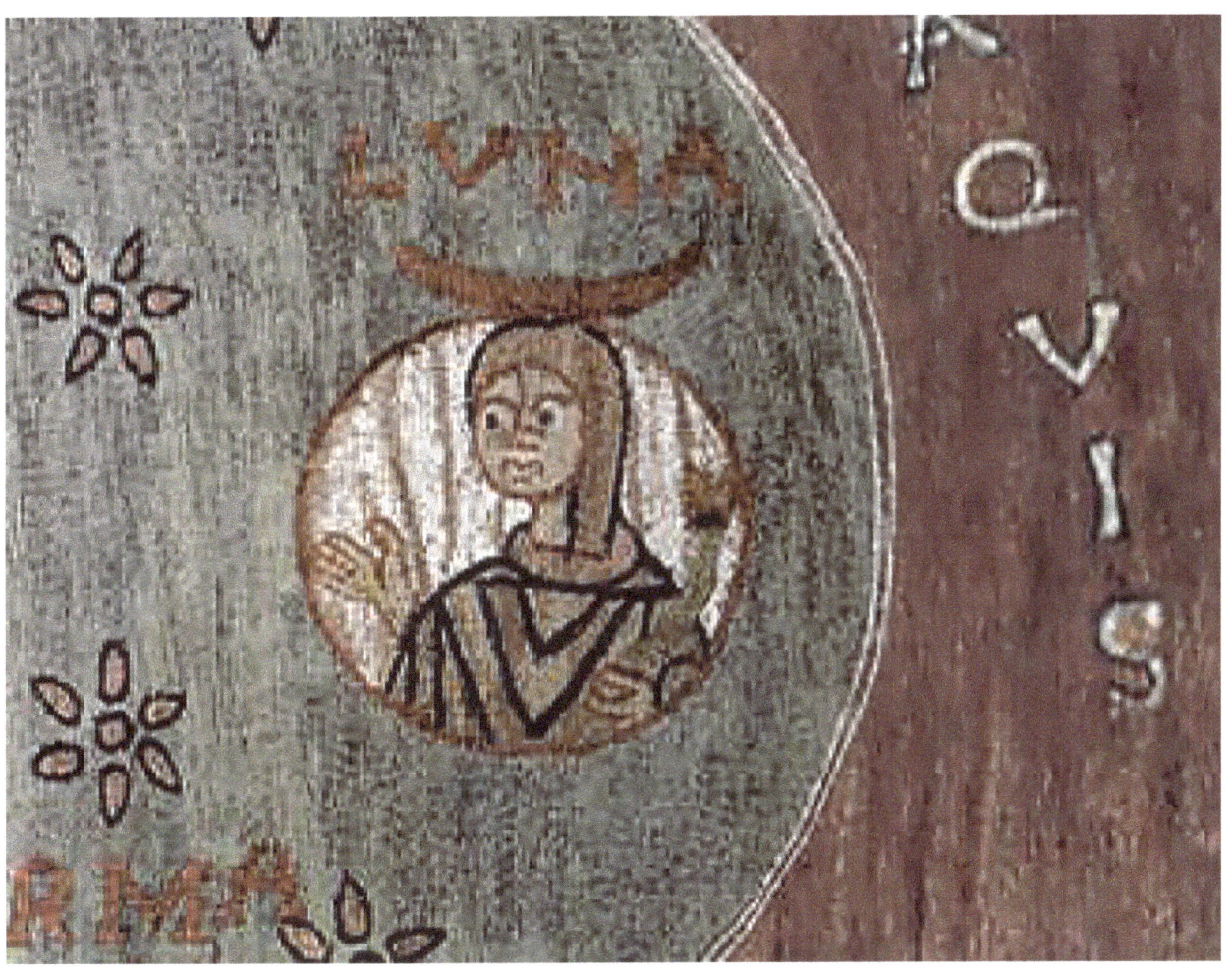

layout emphasizes that life itself is the ultimate goal of creation, of differentiation and of the dynamic process which began at the beginning.

Within the three segments of this picture, we see depicted the diversity and abundance of the archetypes of the animate world. This refers to the second story of creation for it was only life itself which God created out of nothing. "Light" and "darkness," "space" and "time" had their origins in the totality of primal beginnings and its subsequent division, and not through a new act of creation.

To summarize, for every archetype of life the following is valid:

1. It is of both genders, feminine as well as masculine.
2. It has a positive, light side and a negative, dark side.
3. It can manifest itself within the confines of space, but also outside of the confines of space.
4. It can take the form of matter but is also beyond the material realm.
5. It is limited by time, but is also eternal.

The Fifth and Sixth Day of Creation

The three segments of the lower circle are not divided by a white line and can therefore be viewed as being different aspects of one creative act, that is, the emergence of life in all its infinite diversity. In this lower half of the circle, the protarchetype of life is depicted.

In the middle segment we see creatures of the sea and air. The sea creatures represent the more primitive, cold-blooded instincts or archetypes. We could equally well call them body reflexes. Birds, on the other hand, represent a more highly-developed archetypal level; the spiritual reflexes, so to speak.[120] There exists a statue of a Pharaoh of ancient Egypt which shows a king behind whom there is a crocodile with gaping jaws. This refers to his cold-blooded instinct, a reflex-like grabbing and devouring of his opponent. Only by employing such a primitive instinct for self-preservation could he survive the constant threat of power

---

[120] In Sufism, birds represent spiritual inspiration. Bakhtiar, *Sufi*, 37.

struggles and intrigues at his court. Seen from an evolutionary standpoint, the crocodile, being a reptile, is between the fish and the birds.

The mammals of the next segment are divided into one group of domestic animals (horse, cow, sheep, goat, cat, and dog) as well as two wild animals, which are often depicted in Christian allegories, namely, the stag and the unicorn. Behind Adam, and thus invisible to him, two wild mythical beasts are lurking. The mammals shown represent all the higher instincts or archetypes as, for example, the horse which represents the instinct which bears a burden and is creative, and the cow which represents a motherly and nurturing instinct. Then there is the dog which represents an instinct which gives orientation, and the stag and unicorn which are symbols for the spirit and soul of medieval Christianity and can be seen as representing the instinct of individuation.

Adam, the naked primal human being, contemplates the animals, gives them names and searches among them for one of his own kind. Emma Jung and Marie-Louise von Franz offer rich amplifications of the primordial human being and come to the conclusion that Adam represents the "psyche par excellence." "He does not, however, represent only the psyche but, equally, the Self and is therefore 'a visualization of the irrepresentable Godhead.'"[121] Elsewhere, von Franz goes on to qualify her point by saying that Adam represents the preconscious wholeness of the psyche, that he is an image of the living, differentiated psyche in a state of wholeness before the ego-complex has come into being, that is, before consciousness has begun to exist. This state of being corresponds to the psychic situation of animals and, in the sense of a continuum, could be called an early form of the Self. Within this preconscious wholeness of the psyche all behavioral patterns are present, that is to say, all the instincts and archetypes are contained within it. These "move" freely within the psyche and sometimes lead to inner conflicts, to unpredictable behavior or behavioral blocks.[122]

---

[121] Emma Jung and von Franz, *Grail Legend*, 334.

[122] Von Franz, *C. G. Jung*, 81ff. When, for example, a strange animal approaches a brooding bird, this flight or mothering instinct can surface. The bird will then either flee or remain sitting on its eggs. On the depictions of animals on the ceiling of the church in *Zillis*, Rudloff writes: "Whether it is a siren, a nereid, a centaur or a squirrel, these figures all depict processes that occur within the soul, reflecting man's inner life, his drives and his passions." (Translated by Kappes). Rudloff, *Zillis*, 37–38.

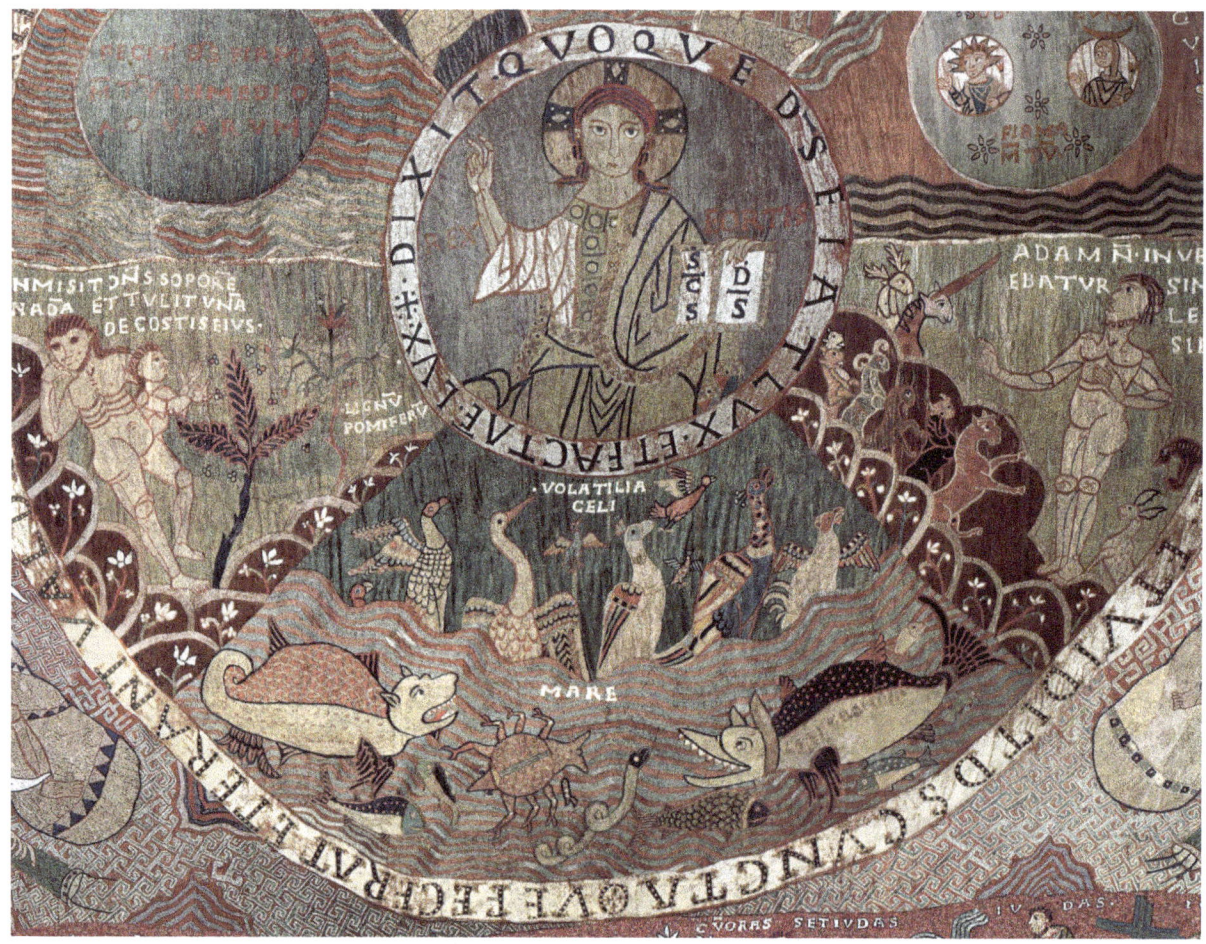

As an image for the totality of the unconscious psyche before the development of consciousness, Adam is thought to incorporate both genders, as is described in the First Book of Moses, Genesis (5:1): "In the day that God created man, in the likeness of God made he him; male and female created he them."

For the great Sufi mystic, Ibn 'Arabi, Adam is a symbol for human beings "at once ephemeral and eternal, a being created perpetual and immortal."[123] That is why: "Adam is the 'unique Spirit' (*an-nafs al-wâhidah*)

---

[123] Ibn al 'Arabi, *Wisdom of the Prophets*, 12.

from which was created the human species."[124] But in the world created by God, there does not yet exist a spiritual being in whom God could see Himself reflected. "Adam became the light itself of this mirror" of the world.[125] Thus, in Sufism too, Adam is an image for the wholeness of the preconscious psyche who, by being the polish on the surface of the mirror, makes it possible for God to see His own reflection in His creation. For it was God's intention to create a perfect human being so that "God becomes conscious of Himself in creation."[126] God taught Adam the names."[127] But to know the name of a thing means to become conscious of the thing in question, as well as being capable of seeing oneself as being separate from it, and not allowing oneself to be governed by it. "By virtue of his knowledge of the names, Adam became master over all created things."[128]

The animals which are both in front of Adam and behind him make this confrontation clear. They represent the inner process of clarifying and distinguishing these different basic psychic patterns, by which we mean the instincts and the archetypes which threaten, but also enliven, Adam's harmony, that is, the harmonious wholeness of his preconscious psyche.

Adam's kneecaps are outlined as circles, with a radial cross in the center of each circle. Knee (Latin: genus; Greek: gonos), gender (Latin: genus) and creative spirit (Latin: genius) point to a shared etymological origin. Further, knee and lap can be used synonymously in the sense of "to sit a child on one's knee," or in one's lap. Lap, however, is a mother's lap in which fruit are able to ripen. According to a Finnish creation myth, a primal bird hatches its primal eggs on the knee of a double-gendered primal being. Therefore, this emphasis on Adam's knees draws attention to the latent creative potential within the preconscious psyche.

In the third segment of this picture, we see Adam asleep while Eve emerges out of his side. We also see the tree of knowledge standing in the middle of paradise, a reference to the fall of man. Only by eating the apple from the tree of knowledge will Adam and Eve become conscious of themselves and thus see themselves as

---

[124] Ibid., 18.
[125] Ibid., 10.
[126] Schimmel, *Mystical Dimensions of Islam*, 224.
[127] Koran, Sure 2:31.
[128] Schimmel, *Mystical Dimensions of Islam*, 188.

being separate from the animals. By their action, a differentiated psychical complex of functioning is aroused, namely, an ego-consciousness. The fact that the tree of knowledge stands at the center of paradise indicates the central significance of this process of gaining consciousness. In creating the tree of knowledge, God foresaw this process of gaining consciousness. In addition, He also created the snake, along with all the other animals in paradise. The snake is a symbol of the Self and thus points toward a process of becoming whole by increasing consciousness. *Thanks* to the fall of man, human kind became conscious and thereby set themselves apart from the animal kingdom. In this sense, we can speak of "felix culpa," the fortunate sin.[129]

Becoming conscious, however, brings with it suffering, for it gives us a sense of responsibility and loneliness. As consciousness increases, an individual becomes increasingly removed from a "participation mystique" with his environment and thereby becomes aware of his own differences and his own limitations. This inevitably leads to his expulsion from paradise forever. That it is Eve, Adam's feminine aspect, who seduces him into self-knowledge means that it is always a female archetype, that is, the anima, which leads man out of his unconscious state and forces upon him a process of becoming conscious by increasing his field of consciousness. Of course, the opposite is also true, that it is always a masculine archetype, the animus, which forces a woman to become more conscious. In everyday life, it is the feminine principle within a man, his feeling-side, which seduces him by means of his passion, his love-affairs, his actions and his relationship problems of every description. As all men are, to some extent, unconscious, a man invariably feels that it is a real, outer woman who causes him trouble. But if he succeeds in withdrawing his projections, then he is able to acknowledge that it is rather his inner woman, his own feminine side, which complicates his life to force him to expand his consciousness in order to overcome the crisis in which he is entangled. The alternative is to remain stuck, to develop somatic problems or to become neurotic. Behind every creative cultural achievement of a man is the female archetype, his anima, the spiritual likeness of his "inspiring woman" (in French, the "femme inspiratrice"). Thus, it is Eve who tempts Adam to eat from the tree of knowledge. Eve, the feminine side of Adam, is therefore the element which furthers the development of the

---

[129] In the liturgy for Good Friday of the Catholic Church, when the Easter candle is being consecrated, reference is made to the felix culpa. The sins of the Adam and Eve are here seen as the precondition for the unfolding of the Redemption story that followed.

preconscious psyche. This makes Eve and the Sapientia Dei analogous images, which, on two different levels, illustrate that the creative impulse emerges from the female principle.

Here the question arises: At which point in history did an ego-consciousness begin to develop in the psyche of primal man? The picture on the right of Adam and the animals is also an image of the first humans of the post-glacial age who scratched and painted images of the animals they encountered on the walls of rocky ledges or caves. At that time, hunters and gatherers followed the seasonal migrations of their prey, such as reindeer, mammoth, woolly-haired cattle, horses, and so on. This can be verified by the numerous hunting camps, for example the one at Nice (a town in Southern France) which was occupied over many years in spring for one to two months.[130] From a psychological point of view, this means that the hunters of the time followed their instincts in the sense of living out an archetypal pattern of behavior. Some individuals (who were most probably the first shamans) discovered for the first time in the history of mankind their own *inner* images, which the extreme introspection and introversion they experienced within the dark depths of their caves induced and which they then painted, drew, or scratched onto the cave walls.

This inner vision was of such an overwhelming nature that, in a very short space of time, there were hundreds of animals depicted on the walls. This was how they first became aware of the fact that the whole wealth of the outer world lies buried within the inner world of a man's soul. The cave paintings are a visual representation of this overwhelming experience, and, with the birth of consciousness, man himself became a creator. At that time, only certain chosen individuals became conscious of their inner wealth of images and, for the first time, were confronted by this discovery. But confrontation presupposes ego-consciousness, which must have been born simultaneously. Even today we can still see traces of the huge emotional storms that this discovery must have engendered within these individuals when we observe the still glowing colors of these paintings, some as old as 30,000 years. But this step forward also meant that such individuals were wrenched out of the unconscious life in which they had lived in total harmony with nature.

In psychological terms, to enter bravely into the dark depths of a cave corresponds to consciously immersing oneself in the unconscious and being confronted by its images. Anyone who has been alone inside a cave

---

[130] For example, the *terra amata* in Nice, probably a hunting station of *Homo erectus*, approx. 300,000 years old.

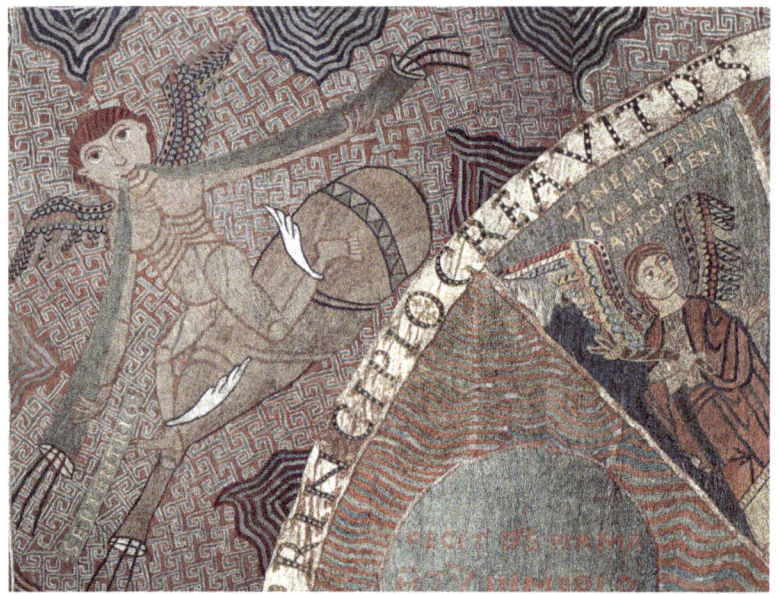

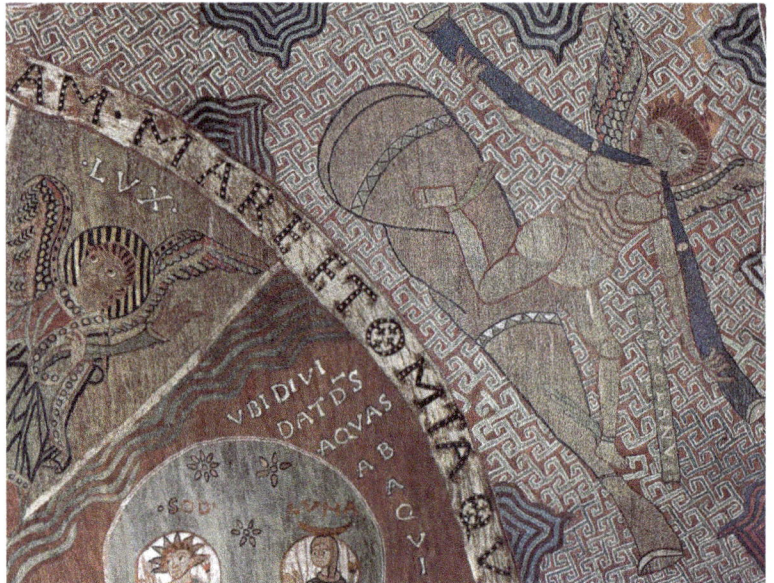

knows of the intense mixed feelings of both curiosity and fear, along with the joyous relief tinged with slight disappointment that one experiences upon seeing the first glimmer of light after one's return to the mouth of the cave. Adam's stance in the right-hand segment of the picture would seem to capture this same tension of being caught between fascination and curiosity. This attitude is equally characteristic of those who, out of an inner need, seek out a confrontation with the inner images of their own soul. Von Franz recognizes this same phenomenon when she points out that every patient in dream analysis with whom she has worked over a longer period of time inevitably expresses a deep longing to forget the realities of the unconscious they have discovered, and to be able to return to so-called "normal life."[131] When ego-awareness begins to manifest itself within an individual, his preconscious wholeness and paradisical innocence are lost forever. And whenever one is gripped by a conscious new

---

[131] Von Franz: Private discussion.

understanding which will change one's life, it is always perceived as being an acutely painful awakening. This is why caves with prehistoric paintings are not just exotic tourist attractions illustrating, perhaps, magical hunting scenes or depicting symbols of fertility. Rather, they are holy places, primeval cathedrals in which individuals had their first experiences of nature gods. Out of such a natural womb Eve was born, and it was she who led Adam to consciousness.

In the Creation Tapestry, the four winds circulate between the world of the beyond and everyday reality. They mediate between the visible and the invisible world. They are the breath of Jehovah, the spirit which animates and gives concrete form to creation. In the Book of Judith (16:14) we can read:

"The whole of creation must serve You for You ordained—and she came into being
You sent Your spirit—and he made all."

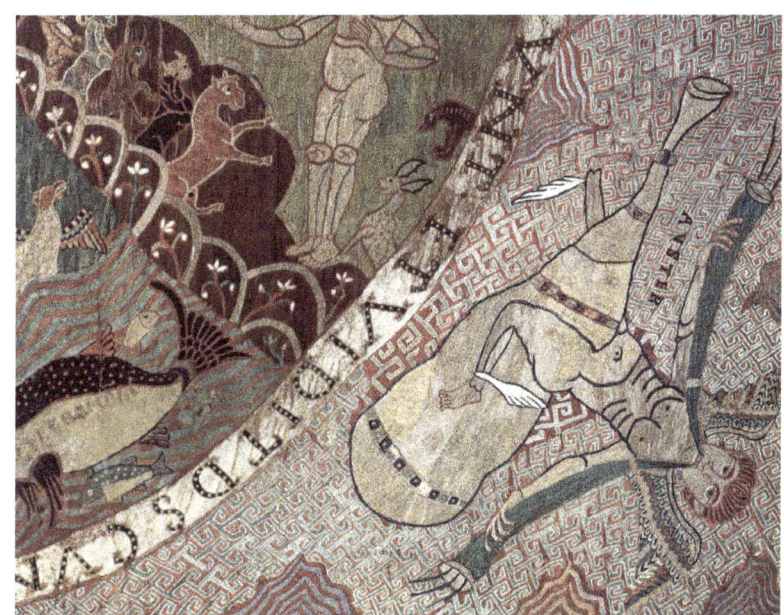

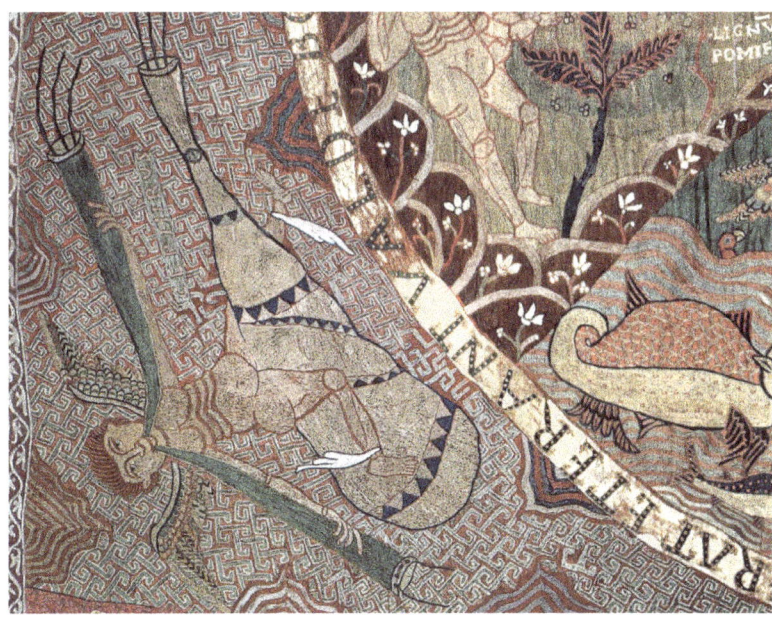

In Hebrew, the same word may be used for "spirit" and "wind," but this "spirit" is thought of as being feminine (see above). In the second creation story,[132] too, God breathes his own breath into man made of clay and thus gives him life. Wind, as the breath or spirit of God, establishes a connection between God's heavenly realm, the *unus mundus*, and concrete reality. Wind gods were viewed as being creator gods or gods of fertility. The mare of Lusitania (a mythological horse) and the Egyptian vulture were both impregnated by a breath of air. The wind is the fertilizing pneuma. Wind is the spirit or hand which transforms thoughts or ideas into concrete reality. It is the dynamic aspect of the unconscious, the spirit, and as such is represented in the Tapestry by the four winds of the four corners of the earth. The wind is the spirit, which mediates between the timeless world of the archetypes and everyday reality. The fact that the winds are blown through pipes, skins or horns, all symbols of the creative organ of the phallus, emphasizes this creative function of the wind.

According to the Sufis, the divine breath pervades the entire universe. It is thought that just as we form syllables and words by exhaling, so too, through the act of exhalation of the divine breath, the visible world is formed. The divine breath has within itself the potential for all forms within the universe and brings life to everything, that is, all forms of nature are realized through divine exhalation. The divine breath is the breath of compassion, and "is essentially the initial act of the metaphysic of love."[133] Love, however, is both the source of, and mystery behind, all of creation and is, therefore, the principle behind all progress, from lust to love, that is, of gaining divine consciousness.

In the Creation Tapestry, the area between the inner circle and the outer border is filled with geometric calligraphy which is arranged in a more or less radial pattern. Over this pattern sweep the winds or the breath of God. This pattern connects the divine inner world of the archetypes with the outer world of concrete reality. The abundant use of arabesques and geometric forms in the calligraphy of Sufism underlines the element of timelessness. Such forms are used to decorate all kinds of surfaces and they represent the word, or logos, out of which God created the world and such geometric structural forms emphasize the progression from the potential to the concrete. Calligraphy is the most sacred art form of the Sufi religion because it is

---

[132] Book of Moses, Gen. 2:7.
[133] Bakhtiar, *Sufi*, 17.

directly connected to the act of creation. It conjures up the eternal spirit of the divine and symbolises the visible body of divine revelation. Through calligraphy, the inanimate becomes animate. One finds it, for example, between the dome (circle) of a mosque and its square floorplan (square) and thus it emphasizes the transition from the transcendental to the immanent. Like the vertical and horizontal threads of a woven tapestry, the vertical and horizontal calligraphic lines represent the relationship between man and God and their relationship within the context of creation. Together they form a whole while representing a process of flowing together. In addition, they indicate the active and passive qualities in all things. The geometric structure of vertical and horizontal lines form a creative rhythm that is perceived by the soul of a mystic. These vibrations bring about changes within his soul as he makes his journey toward the divine.

The Sufi mystic "knows" that inherent in every passing moment is the destruction and creation of the universe. The world is in constant motion. The flow, however, is so well-ordered and continuous, and is so governed by natural laws, that man is not aware of this motion and perceives the world as being constant. This process of eternal renewal is something which only those people who live in close contact with their own Self can recognize. The arabesque patterns in carpets represent this thought of constant flow.[134] Ibn 'Arabi had this to say about it: "The wonder of wonders is that the human form and all other created things are in a perpetual process of ascending. How splendid is God's description of the universe, and of its perpetual renewal with each Divine Breath."[135]

The geometric calligraphy between the inner circle and outer square of the Creation Tapestry forms a pattern of lines which correspond to a device normally used in Islam to express the connection between God and man, between eternal existence and concrete reality. This calligraphy is woven into the Creation Tapestry at the very spot where the divine existence forms the background for concrete reality. Such calligraphy is an iconographical element which demonstrates a direct Islamic influence on the creation of the Tapestry.

There is yet another pictorial element which testifies to an Islamic influence, namely, the vine and leaf motif framing the whole Tapestry and the individual square pictures that form its border. As far as we can tell, these are surrounded by fine red bands with regularly occurring wave-like vines bearing leaves threading through them.

---

[134] Ibid.
[135] Bakhtiar, *Sufi*, 17.

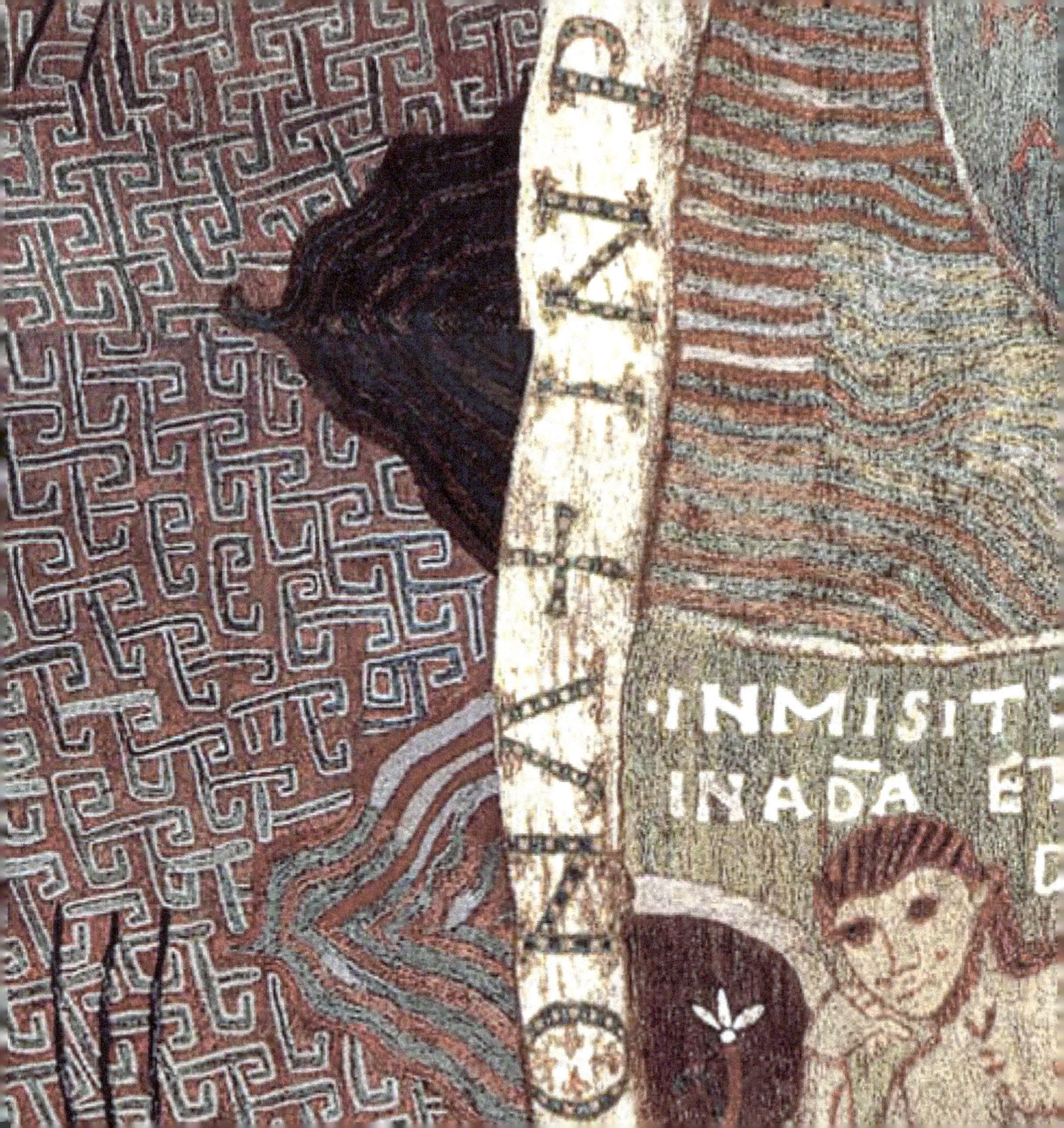

·INMISIT
INADA E
D

Such border motifs are frequent in Islamic art and are widespread. In a more or less abstract form, they are to be seen in pictures and manuscripts,[136] in mosaics and textiles,[137] with flowers in full bloom, with buds and with leaves. Toward the end of the 12th century, mystical Sufi poetry regarded every flower as being "a tongue to praise God; every leaf and petal is a book in which God's wisdom can be read."[138] They are a part of the wealth of arabesques and geometrical calligraphic forms that all refer to the divine emanations in the here and now.

If one sees the Creation Tapestry as being an attempt on the part of its creators to express Christianity's defining boundaries in the midst of what was, in many ways, a superior Islamic culture, then it should come as no surprise to see that, to a large extent, iconographic elements from the Islamic culture are absent. Nevertheless, in choosing a mandala to be the basic pattern of the Tapestry, its creators made use of an Islamic design technique in order to express their own different Christian image of God in contrast to the more abstract Islamic one.[139] Much supports the assumption of a close connection between Islam and Christianity at the time of the Tapestry's creation; for example, the wealth of statements that, although expressed in different ways (that is, pictorially depicted in the Creation Tapestry in contrast to the use of symbols, artistically formulated and presented in a highly differentiated way in Islamic Sufism), mean the same thing.

Bearing this in mind, it is my view that there is no valid argument to refute the hypothesis of the Tapestry having been created on Christian soil in Spain. Rather, in my opinion, there is much to support the argument of the Tapestry having been created within a context of close spiritual contact between its creators and Islam. Indeed, it can be seen as being their own response to the challenge of Islamic Spain.

In the Creation Tapestry, the four principal winds are related to the four points of the compass, with the north and east winds being on top. What could this orientation to the north-east mean?

According to Hildegard of Bingen, the winds from the four corners of the earth embody the powerful law-abiding energies of the cosmos: "The four cardinal winds support the firmament under and above the sun and hold it together. They enclose, as with a cloak, the entire circle, that is, from the lowest to the highest

---

[136] Bakhtiar, *Sufi*, 83 (Hand-written manuscript on the life of Mohammed from 16th century); and ibid., 85 (Hand-written manuscript of Khamseh, from around 1410).
[137] Cf. for example ibid., 75 (Qalamkar cloths, 20th century), 50–51 (prayer carpet, 19th century), 63 (garden carpet, from around 1700).
[138] Schimmel, *Mystical Dimensions of Islam*, 308.
[139] Cf. chapter "Its Meaning as a Tapestry," and "The Tapestry as a Mandala."

part of the firmament. The east wind embraces the air and pours a very mild dew over everything dry. The west wind mixes with the floating clouds, to keep the waters from erupting. The south wind keeps the fire under its control and prevents it from burning everything. The north wind controls the outer darkness so that it does not exceed its measure."[140]

It is with the help of the four winds and their constant permeation, which brings about the world's rotation, that God keeps the cosmic structure of the world in harmony. But the winds also bear influence upon individuals, for they make a person stronger or weaker, and if he is wise, with the help of the wind, he is able to bring harmony to both his body and his soul.[141]

Hildegard of Bingen is focussed upon a united world made up of both the microcosmos and the macrocosmos. She ascribes the following attributes to the four principal winds: the east wind personifies the wet-warm wind, the air, spring, the sanguine temperament, and by knowing goodness, the human soul looks to the east; the west wind, however, points toward all that is bad, and is the dry-cold wind, the earth, autumn and represents a melancholic temperament; the south wind means the warm-dry wind, fire, summer and the choleric temperament; and finally, the north wind expresses the cold-wet wind, water, winter, and a phlegmatic temperament.[142]

The cosmology of medieval man included cartography. His earthly existence reached to the edge of the world where huge mountain ranges were believed to exist, just as is depicted in the Creation Tapestry where numerous pointed mountains exist between everyday reality and the circle of creation.

The most widespread map of Christian cartographers was the so-called T-map which was set out like a mandala.[143] A full circle encompassed the then known continents of Asia, Africa, and Europe. As a rule, the map's orientation was toward the east, that is, east was at the top, and the early Christian church shared this orientation toward the east. It is in the east that the sun rises to make its journey across the sky. Paradise was believed to be located in the east and Christianity had its origins in the east. Similarly, it is believed that Christ's Second Coming will come out of the east. In contrast to this, the maps of the Greeks were of a

---

[140] Hildegard of Bingen, *Natural Philosophy and Medicine*, 26.
[141] Ibid., 26ff.
[142] Ibid.
[143] Legner, *Monumenta Annonis*, 112. For Kosmas Indikopleustes (6th century), the earth had a rectangular form surrounded by ocean, with wind-blowing angels at each corner; cf. Rudloff, *Zillis*, 32.

northward orientation, and this was adopted by modern cartographers. Arabian cartography, however, bears a southward orientation which meant that on their maps, south was at the top.[144]

In her tremendous cosmic visions, Hildegard of Bingen saw a divine plan:

"For I who inhabit all the ends of the world, I manifested all my works in the east and south and west. However, the fourth part, in the north, I kept void; neither sun nor moon give their light there. That is why in that place, beyond the structured world, there hell exists, which neither has a roof above nor ground below. That is the place of darkness, which, however, serves a purpose for all the glorious givers of light. Because, how else could light be recognized, if not with the help of darkness? And how would one know about darkness if not with the help of the brightness of my light-bearing servants. In the light one perceives the working of God. In the darkness one becomes aware of a distance from God, where light does not reach."[145]

That is why in the Creation Tapestry, Lucifer, the Angel of Darkness, inhabits the north whereas the Angel of Light dwells in the east. Jung wrote a cultural/historical presentation of the various interpretations applicable to the north and summarized by saying:

"Ancient history gives us a divided picture of the region to the north: it is the seat of the highest gods and also of the adversary; thither men direct their prayers, and from thence blows an evil pneuma, the Aquilo, 'by the name whereof is to be understood the evil spirit'; and finally, it is the navel of the world and at the same time hell."[146]

North-east is centered at the top of the Creation Tapestry. In the 11th and 12th centuries, mankind stood at the threshold of a new orientation when the original orientation toward the east was changing into one toward the north, or at least such a change was in the air. In addition, it is worth noticing that the east wind is depicted as having lost its strength: the airbag on which it rides is somewhat deflated and it is the only wind of the four which is not blowing. This, it would seem, indicates that Christianity's orientation toward the east has been worn out for there are no longer any spiritual impulses to be expected from this direction. Furthermore,

---

[144] Ibid.
[145] Hildegard of Bingen, *Hildegard von Bingen*, 125–26. (Translated by Kappes)
[146] Jung, *Aion*, vol. 9/II, *GW*, §§ 192, and §§ 158ff.

a Christian orientation towards the north set up a direct contrast to the Arabs whose maps were invariably oriented toward the south.

But what new impulses could be expected to come out of the north, from where the wind blows the strongest? *Adam Scotus* imagined that to the north lay a frightful dragon's head, the source of all evil. Out of its mouth and nose came three different kinds of vapour or smoke representing the three great uncertainties of good and evil, of truth and falsehood, of propriety and impropriety. Consequently, the north is linked to the sins of unconsciousness, as *Clemens Romanus* points out.[147]

But Lucifer, the bringer of light (Lux means light), also dwells in the north, the very same Lucifer who, in the Garden of Eden, had already tempted the first human couple to become conscious. Thus, "north" is a symbol for the two naturally-opposing tendencies of the psyche, namely, that of remaining unconscious, on the one hand, and of becoming conscious, on the other. Ultimately, though, the real sin of mankind is clearly stated:

"Man, if indeed thou knowest what thou doest, thou art blessed; but if thou knowest not, thou art cursed, and a transgressor of the law."[148]

According to the Sufi mystics, the figure of Iblis is not just a symbol of total disobedience toward Allah but also, because of his one-eyedness, Iblis is a symbol of one-sided intellectualism, devoid of all love for its creator. As a result, Iblis, or Satan, became a tragic figure, one who is lost, lonely and without any hope, who feels a deep longing to be defeated by "the perfect man," crushed in order to be redeemed at last.[149] Thus, he is the dark which longs for light, the outcast who wants to be accepted. He represents the contents of the unconscious which want to enter consciousness but are either not accepted by it or only at a painful cost. As von Franz has so impressively shown, creation myths are always also a portrayal of human attempts toward consciousness. In other words, by means of multifarious images, creation myths sketch the fundamental creative patterns in the human psyche out of which consciousness is born and expanded upon throughout a human life.[150]

---

[147] Ibid., § 158.
[148] Jung, *Psychology and Religion*, vol. 11, *CW*, § 696, fn 6: An apocryphal insertion at Luke 6:4.
[149] Schimmel, *Mystical Dimensions of Islam*, 196.
[150] Von Franz, *Creation Myths*.

PHYSICS AND DEPTH PSYCHOLOGY: Modern Approaches to Wholeness?

Is it possible to make a connection between the concepts we have deduced from the images of the Creation Tapestry and modern science by relating them to psyche, space, matter, time and life? Nowadays, the field of nuclear physics, and related subjects, is largely (if not exclusively) governed by the concepts of symmetry and polarity. In his studies of the psyche, Jung experienced similar phenomena. As in the natural sciences where, ultimately, any polarity can be described as a symmetry, similarly the notion gradually and repeatedly suggested itself to Jung that, in the realm of the psyche, a secret convergence of the poles was imaginable. This was particularly true for the opposites of psyche and matter.[151] Therewith, Jung discovered a new principle which behaved in a complementary manner to causality and implied a final, meaningfully-related aspect, namely, the principle of synchronicity.[152]

With his interest in synchronistic phenomena, Jung concentrated on those rare exceptions which do not comply with the rules of scientific experimentation. Jung writes:

"The experimental method of inquiry aims at establishing regular events which can be repeated. Consequently, unique or rare events are ruled out of account. Moreover, the experiment imposes limiting conditions on nature, for its aim is to force her to give answers to questions devised by man. Every answer of nature is therefore more or less influenced by the kind of questions asked, and the result is always a hybrid

---

[151] Von Franz, *C. G. Jung*, 80–81.
[152] Jung, *Structure and Dynamics*, vol. 8, *CW*; von Franz, *Divination and Synchronicity*.

product. The so-called 'scientific view of the world' based on this can hardly be anything more than a psychologically biased partial view which misses out all those by no means unimportant aspects that cannot be grasped statistically."[153]

What do we understand by synchronicity or synchronistic phenomena? By synchronistic phenomena or synchronicities we mean the chance convergence of events from two or more independent causal chains which are characterized by their taking place almost simultaneously as well as by the meaning which they convey to the person, or people, involved in such a chance happening. Jung also speaks of meaningful coincidences or similarities and claims that synchronicity is a principle of acausally-connected events. He believes that "synchronicity in the narrow sense is only a particular instance of general acausal orderedness."[154] We also come across such chance happenings in physics, for example, in the form of physical half-life or the speed of light. These measurements are absolute factors based on causes seemingly beyond our knowledge. They are acausal "just-so" arrangements.

A further quotation from Jung states:

"Synchronicity is no more baffling or mysterious than the discontinuity of physics. It is only the ingrained belief in the sovereign power of causality that creates intellectual difficulties and makes it appear unthinkable that causeless events exist or could ever occur. Meaningful coincidences are thinkable as pure chance. ... But the more they multiply and the greater and more exact the correspondence is, the more their probability sinks and their unthinkability increases, until they can no longer be regarded as pure chance but, for lack of a causal explanation, have to be thought of as meaningful arrangements. ... Their 'inexplicability' is not due to the fact that the cause is unknown, but to the fact that a cause is not even thinkable in intellectual terms."[155]

It is always the meaningful component which connects unrelated events and turns them into a synchronistic experience. Meaning, however, is generally a subjective experience for it is up to the individual to decide what is meaningful and what is not.

---

[153] Jung, *Structure and Dynamics*, vol. 8, *CW* § 821.
[154] Ibid., § 965.
[155] Ibid., § 967.

Jung, however, took the significant step of detaching the factor of meaning involved in synchronicity from the subjective judgement of the individual and elevating it by making it an independent principle. "Synchronicity postulates a meaning which is *a priori* in relation to human consciousness and apparently exists outside man."[156] *Jaffé* comments on the same subject:

"When a synchronicity is experienced, it is not a question of giving it a subjective interpretation. Rather, it is a question of making its objective, a priori meaning conscious, or to put it more exactly, of discovering such a meaning."[157]

Going hand-in-hand with the above is Jung's discovery that there is "in the unconscious something like a priori knowledge" or an "absolute knowledge." Schopenhauer, who was Jung's model for his work on synchronicity, speaks of a "dreamy omniscience." "Accordingly, synchronistic phenomena are not only to be understood as being an invasion into space and time within the spacelessness and timelessness of the unconscious, but also as being manifestations of an a priori meaning and of an absolute knowledge, or, as it has been called, a pre-existent knowing."[158] Jung, together with the physicist Wolfgang Pauli, added a fourth principle to the already-existing triad of classical systems in physics (that is, of space, time, and causality) in full knowledge that only absolute necessity justified such an addition. Justification for this necessity lies in the fact that the phenomenon of meaningful coincidence does not fit into the existing system of natural sciences based, as they are, on causality. A system, however, which is not able to accommodate essential human facts of experience needs to be extended.

Medieval philosophical theory accepted the idea of all things being interrelated ("the correspondentia" [*Leibniz*]) as self-evident. But this theory increasingly lost ground with the emergence of natural science and its dictatorial view of causality, until finally, knowledge of the world as a totality was forgotten altogether. Some current problematical postulations and findings in physics and biology, as well as in psychology and

---

[156] Ibid., § 942.
[157] Jaffé, *Jungs Welt*, 74. (Translated by Kappes)
[158] Ibid., 75. (Translated by Kappes)

parapsychology, which do not accord with a causal viewpoint, indicate a need for a revision of the natural scientific standpoint.[159]

In ancient China, the principle of synchronicity was the "modus operandi" for viewing the world and its history. In those days, people knew that man's behavior, the microcosmos, stood in direct relationship to the macrocosm.[160] Ultimately, the principle of synchronicity refers to a transcendental interrelatedness of the whole world.

In their paper "Synchronicity: an acausal connecting principle,"[161] Jung and Pauli reached a consensus on classifying synchronicity. By adding the principle of synchronicity to the natural scientific triad of space/time/causality, which are the confines of our Western understanding of the world, Jung elevated this triad into a quaternio. Following a suggestion by Pauli, this quaternio was thus able to accommodate both the postulates of depth psychology as well those of modern physics. As matter is a form of energy and, ultimately, so is psyche, we must therefore subsume material and psychic phenomena as being indestructible energy. According to such a model, psyche and matter can be connected by means of synchronicity, as is demonstrated in the inner circle of the Creation Tapestry. In contrast to causality, which is the mediating factor between space and time and is always bound to the space/time system, synchronicity is causality's complement, joining psyche and matter.

For the moment, it would therefore seem that from the mandala of the inner circle of the Creation Tapestry we can ascertain the following points:

1. Life exists within a quaternio of space, time, matter, and psyche.
2. Life is based upon the retrospective principle of causality as well as the forward-looking principle of synchronicity in equal measure.

---

[159] Isler, *Sennenpuppe*, 10–11.
[160] Von Franz, *Projection and Re-Collection*.
[161] Jung, *Structure and Dynamics*, vol. 8, *CW*.

3. By observing the phenomena of life without taking into account both psyche and synchronicity (as is attempted in natural science today where only space, time, matter, and causality are considered), one cannot do justice to all the phenomena of life.

Our perception of space and time, as well as psyche and matter, is based upon general human experience. In essence, we all experience space, time, psyche, and matter in the same way. But these individual experiences are subject to a general psychic pattern, a fundamental archetype, the protoarchetype. Like all archetypes, this protoarchetype is, according to Jung, of a psychoid nature, that is, it's nature is bound neither by psyche/matter nor by space/time. Rather, the protoarchetype can manifest itself concretely in space and in time, in psyche as well as in matter. Space and time are connected by causality. All that we are able to recognize as cause and effect takes place within the framework of time and space. Psyche and matter, on the other hand, are connected by a different principle. Their connection is synchronicity, that is, there are moments in our lives which are rarely experienced consciously in which an archetype manifests in both matter (in the form of an outer event) as well as in our psyche (in the form of a dream, a fantasy or a vision).[162]

The same is true for steps taken in biological evolution. It is likely that once a step upward in our evolution has led to higher development, the genetic code rearranges itself in a multitude of single basic sequences with the aim of achieving something new that has a purpose or significance. Yet these mutations cannot be distinguished from evolutionary occurrences that happen by chance. Only their evolutionary purposefulness or meaningfulness establishes their synchronistic nature. Thus, a step made in the evolutionary process is subject to an archetype. In this way, a possibility that, up until now, has remained hidden, manifests itself in space, time, matter, and in a causal event, as, for example, when the mechanism of "natural selection" becomes activated.[163] In such a case we could speak of molecular synchronicity!

Von Franz writes about this:

---

[162] In recent times, astrology is also paying more attention to synchronicity, for example: Ring, *Astrologie ohne Aberglaube*; or Greene, *Astrology of Fate*, especially the chapter on fate and synchronicity.
[163] Etter, "Evolution und Tiefenpsychologie."

"The most essential and certainly the most impressive thing about synchronistic occurrences, the thing which really constitutes their numinosity, is the fact that in them the duality of soul and matter seems to be eliminated. They are therefore an empirical indication of an ultimate unity of all existence, which Jung, using the terminology of medieval natural philosophy, called the *unus mundus*. In medieval philosophy this concept designates *the potential pre-existent model of creation in the mind of God,* in accordance with which God later produced the creation."[164]

"Jung saw an anticipation of the concept of the *collective unconscious* in these medieval calculations. In the collective unconscious, too, experience shows that everything appears to be more or less connected with everything else in a unity, although certain archetypes emerge with relative distinctiveness, around which individual images cluster. The way in which the multiplicity of the collective unconscious is ordered in a unity is revealed with special clarity in the mandala symbolism. 'The mandala symbolizes, by its central point, the ultimate unity of all archetypes as well as of the multiplicity of the phenomenal world, and is therefore the empirical equivalent of the metaphysical concept of a *unus mundus.*'"[165]

"Microphysics is feeling its way into the unknown side of matter, just as complex psychology is pushing forward into the unknown side of the psyche. But this much we do know beyond all doubt, that empirical reality has a transcendental background. The common background of microphysics and depth psychology is as much physical as psychic and therefore neither, but rather a third thing, a neutral nature which can at most be grasped in hints since in essence it is transcendental."[166]

Dorn describes the experience of the *unus mundus* as the opening of a "window on eternity" or of an "air-hole" into the eternal world. And, in fact, an experience of the Self helps a person to extricate himself from the stifling prison of a conscious image of the world that is too narrow, so that he can be open to the transcendental and so that, at the same time, the transcendental can touch and move him. It can be compared with the sartori experience of Zen Buddhism, or with the samadhi of certain Eastern teachings, or with an

---

[164] Von Franz, *C. G. Jung,* 247.
[165] Ibid., 248: Quotation of Jung, *Mysterium Coniunctionis,* vol. 14/II, *CW,* § 661.
[166] Ibid., 249: Quotaion of Jung, *Mysterium Coniunctionis,* vol. 14/II, *CW,* §§ 767–69.

awakening to the Tao in China. Our finite human life has meaning only when it is related to the infinite through the "window on eternity."[167]

In "the symbolism of mandalas [—in general and also in the mandala in the Creation Tapestry of Gerona—] the unity of all cosmic existence is more to the fore [...] as an irrepresentable background to the world. A genuine experience of this *unus mundus* was in the past almost always hoped for as an event which would happen only at the time of death or after death. Certain ancient Egyptian liturgies for the dead, for example, depict in moving language the way in which the deceased becomes one with all the gods and all the matter of the World-All and is thus finally united within the primordial father, Nun, the primordial ocean itself, from which the world was created. The one who has died can then pass effortlessly through all crude material objects and 'go into and out of all forms.' In Chinese Taoism this happens to him who has become one with the *unus mundus*: 'He walks on air and clouds; he rides on sun and moon and travels beyond the world. Life and death cannot change his self'." He understands how "to make the innermost essence of nature his own, and to let himself be moved by the changing primordial powers, to wander there, where there are no boundaries."[168]

If we accept the four protoarchetypes of psyche, space, matter, and time as being emanations from the primordial origin of the world, then there must be *four* approaches to the existence of the world; via the psyche, via matter, via space, and via time. The latter two seem to me to be made transparent within the context of Einstein's paradoxical theory of space and time. Possibly, one can also recognize them in the theory of "black holes" in astrophysics. These black holes are clusters of stars which have become unstable and have imploded, causing their mass to become so dense as to prohibit any emission of information. Even light can no longer escape, and thus they manifest as black holes. This extrapolation leads one to presume that, at the end of such an implosion, time and space cease to exist and all matter subject to such a force of gravity is transformed into energy.

---

[167] Ibid., 250.
[168] Ibid., 251: Quotations from Dschuang Dsi, *Das wahre Buch vom südlichen Blütenland* (Jena: Eugen Diederichs, 1912), 19, 4.

Both the archetypes of the collective unconscious as well as the special theory of relativity prove (to Jung's own surprise) that something seems to exist beyond, or outside of, time. Jung spoke of the relativity of the space/time continuum in reference to the deeper layers of the psyche, the psychoid systems. Of this, he wrote:

"The archetypal world is 'eternal', i.e., outside time, and it is everywhere, as there is no space under [...] archetypal conditions."[169] And he goes on to ask, "shouldn't we give up the time-space categories altogether when we are dealing with psychic existence? It might be that psyche should be understood as *unextended intensity* and not as a body moving with time. One might assume the psyche gradually rising [...] transcending for instance the velocity of light and thus irrealizing the body. In the light of this view the brain might be a transformer station, in which the relatively infinite tension or intensity of the psyche proper is transformed into perceptible frequencies or 'extensions.'"[170]

In this case the psyche would be without the dimension of space and time. Jung called this idea a speculation. In von Franz's view, however, this speculation has increasingly proved itself to be the key to understanding many facts which have been discovered since then.[171]

Indeed, the collective unconscious is not only a psychic structure innate to all human beings but is also "an omnipresent continuum," an "extended present." If something happens within point A which has an effect upon, or involves, the collective unconscious in some way, then this event has happened everywhere. In this way, space and time become relativized, that is to say, they exist and do not exist simultaneously. Thus, the principle of synchronicity does away with the age-old problem of psyche versus matter.[172]

In a lecture on matter, Schrödinger points out "that everything—*really everything*—is simultaneously particle and field," and he goes on to say, "the difficulty, which is equal in all cases, of combining these two widely different characteristics in one mental picture is still today the major obstacle that makes our image of matter so variable and uncertain."[173] In 1905, Einstein had already come to the conclusion "that energy possesses

---

[169] Jung, *Letters*, vol. 2, 46.
[170] Ibid., 45.
[171] Von Franz, *Psyche and Matter*, 162.
[172] Etter, "Psyche und Materie."
[173] Schrödinger, "Our image of matter," 43.

mass and that mass is energy, that they are one and the same."[174] Because of this identity of mass and energy, particles themselves must be seen as being Plank's energy quanta. Thus, one cannot think of single particles as being well-defined, enduring organisms. Schroedinger says,[175] "They [molecules] can at the most perhaps be thought of as more or less temporary creations within the wave field, whose structure and structural variety, in the widest sense of the word, are so clearly and sharply determined by means of wave laws as they recur always in the same manner, that much takes place *as if* they were a permanent material reality." On the whole, mass can be looked upon as being a statistical effect, supported by the "law of the large number."[176]

Elsewhere Schroedinger refers to matter as being a term to denote an interconnected "chain" of events which are sequential in time. In this way, matter is ultimately an expression of energy in space and time. The same is true for the psyche which, in our view, is ultimately psychic energy manifested in space and time. According to Schroedinger, this "interconnected chain of events" is governed by an energetic phenomenon which can realize itself in the psyche or in matter. This process corresponds to the dynamic aspect of the archetypes which Jung calls psychoid because they are neither psychic nor material, but are both. Archetypes can become both activated and constellated without our being able to recognize a reason for their doing so.

When Jung talks of the relationship between psyche and matter as being a permanent, reciprocal mirroring of each other, we might venture to ask the question whether the relationship between time and space is a similar one. Von Franz has demonstrated the relationship between number and time, and she refers to number as being a part of the original archetype of order.[177] Time is valid only in a relative sense, a fact which has been demonstrated by depth psychology as well as in quantum physics. Time is irrepresentable and is given expression by means of numbers. The same is true for space. It, too, is valid only in a relative sense, as both physics and depth psychology have shown, and like time, space, too, is irrepresentable and is measured by numbers.

---

[174] Ibid., 46.
[175] Ibid., 56.
[176] Ibid.
[177] Von Franz, *Number and Time*.

In this way, causality, which is bound to space and time, is connected to the archetype of number, the principle of existing order. Synchronicity, on the other hand, has to do with an energy which is aiming at some goal, and is therefore connected to the principle of prospective order. Causal processes increase chaos because they are governed by the law of increasing entropy.[178] Meaningful or final processes, on the other hand, are "negentrope," that is, they create order.

From the perspective of the gods and the Beyond, the realization of reality in the here and now means an ever-increasing degree of disorder. But when reality is viewed from the standpoint of this world, it would seem that the real world with its animated nature is striving toward an ever-increasing degree of order. Toward the end of his life, Darwin surmised the existence of a force in nature similar to the force of gravity in physics which ultimately pushes nature ahead to further development.[179] Accordingly, the act of creation would correspond to both a division and a disintegration of the divine chaos in order to bring about a new divine order through space, time, matter, and psyche of the real world, that is, by means of our living world, with nature and its drive toward higher development.

When, however, modern man believes himself to be the "God of love" with the power to control the world's development, then he has cut himself off from his own roots in nature with the result that his behavior wreaks havoc upon his natural environment, destroying what his instincts tell him is most valuable.[180]

In the pictures that form the frame of the Creation Tapestry, we see the emanation of the divine into reality depicted, "a still-life of God" represented in the multiplicity of our world as we know it. Here, in squares, we see the annual cycle of human activity. Such activity takes place within the framework of time. This is why Annus, who is a personification of the concept of the year, which was the largest unit of time known in the Middle Ages, is enthroned in the upper center of the frame, flanked by four quarters, which represent

---

[178] In physics, entropy is a "measure of disorder." The entropy of a closed system can never decrease because conditions of higher probability never change into conditions of lower probability (Theory of entropy).

[179] Wille, *Darwins Weltanschauung*, 16.

[180] In this respect, a Sioux chief who was visiting an art gallery for the first time, brilliantly expressed the "strange wisdom of the white man" seen from his own more natural standpoint, by saying: "He destroys the forest that has stood proud and tall for centuries; he tears the womb out of Mother Earth and spoils the clear streams and rivers; he mercilessly destroys the irreplaceable paintings and friezes made by God in every imaginable way, and then he smears a canvas with some color and calls it a masterpiece." Schwarzer Hirsch, *heilige Pfeife*, 221. (Translated by Kappes)

the seasons. This everyday reality extends from matter to psyche and takes place within space. Synchronicity and causality are the intermediating principles of this reality. Because synchronistic phenomena mediate creative acts within time, they are thus expressions of *continuous creation, of creation beyond time which is realized in the here and now*. In this way, the story of creation in Genesis as well as its pictorial representation in the Creation Tapestry both point to the eternal aspects of creation, for creation took place not only at the dawn of time, but, in a true Augustinian sense, is always taking place (for it was St. Augustine who said that for God, everything happens simultaneously). *Creation manifests itself continuously as synchronistic moments both for an individual as well as for the collective, from the moment of conception until death. Such synchronistic moments are empirical indications of the unity of all existence, of the unus mundus, and are essentially manifestations of a "creatio ex inhilo."*

From conception until death, our real life is acted out against the background of the above-mentioned four-dimensional field. At the moment of conception, a previously hidden possibility of a life manifests itself as a psycho-physical entity in space and in time. The fertilized egg is, on the one hand, the causal consequence of sexual intercourse and its physiology. On the other hand, it is presumably also a synchronistic event, in so far as the matter of the genetic material distributes itself by chance in such a manner that a psycho-physical unity is able to form itself within the individual. Our life in the reality of the here and now is always unfolding within the web of this four-dimensional net of relationship and is equally determined by the two principles of causality and synchronicity.

By the procreation of higher life, the precondition to the moment of conception is the existence of an egg and a sperm. Fertilization may or may not be successful, that is, a male-female/destructive-constructive primordial pattern pre-exists every act of procreation. At the moment of fertilization, a new life emerges out of the irrepresentable condition of pre-existence into space and time and enters the reality of the here and now as a psycho-physical entity. The synchronistic component of this event is the *"chance"* meeting of a particular egg with a particular sperm while the *causal* component is the physiological process that is set in motion, for example the merging of the two cells, the growth of a new membrane around the egg, which is impenetrable to other sperm, and so on. This example should illustrate that an act of creation in the here and now (space and time) takes place as a psycho-physical reality, involving both causal and synchronistic phenomena.

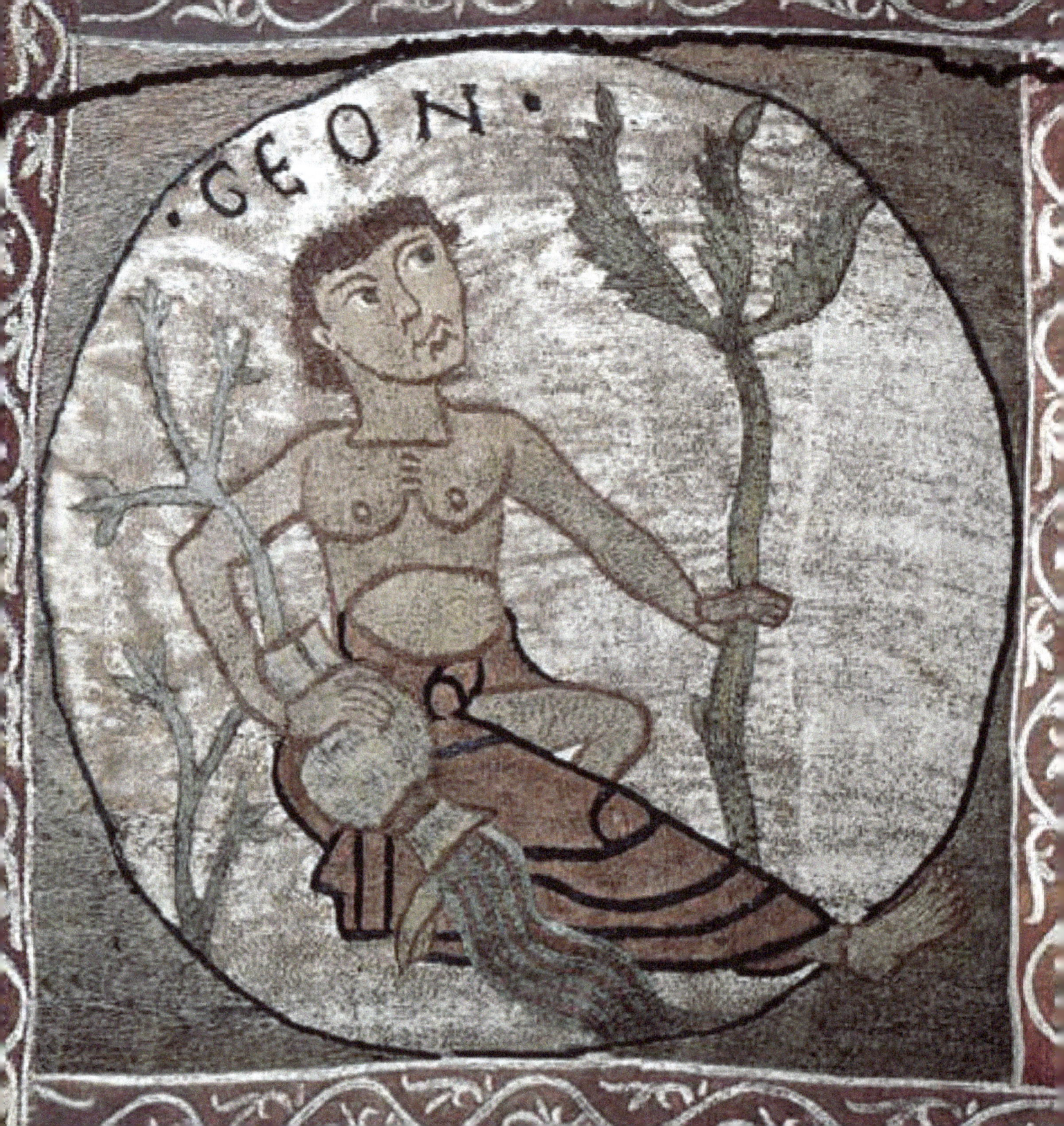

EVERYDAY LIFE AS DEPICTED IN THE BORDER OF THE TAPESTRY

According to Champeaux and Sterckx, in medieval Christian pictorial art the transition from circle to square as shown in the Creation Tapestry is generally interpreted as being a symbol of creation. Underlying this movement from circle to square is, in essence, an archetype which manifests itself in a ritual transition from the center of a thing to a circle, and then from a circle to a square. This symbolic language is universal and has been used throughout man's history. Romanesque architecture is, in the last analysis, also based upon this archetype.[181]

All creation in the Bible emanates from a center, from God, but from a God about whom John (1:18) says: "No man hath seen God at any time." This inextensible center, which is motionless and outside of space and time and outside of psyche and matter is symbolized by the center of the earthly paradise, where the tree of knowledge of good and evil and the tree of life grow. Either flowing out from this center or flowing toward it from the four corners of the Garden of Eden are the four rivers of paradise: the Gihon, the Pison, the Tigris, and the Euphrates. It is these rivers of paradise that form for the first time the cross of the first quaternio, thereby giving expression to the differentiated wholeness of the creation process. Symbolically speaking, this cross mediates between the circle and the square.[182]

---

[181] For example, Champeaux and Sterckx, *Monde des Symbols*, 107.
[182] Ibid.

The four rivers of paradise are thought to be identical with the primal waters that carry the creative power of God. They have the ability to cleanse and to fertilize.[183] Moreover, the rivers of paradise are thought to be identical with both the *mysterium* of Eden, the one river which divides into four sources, as well as with Oceanos, the river which surrounds the earth like a ring. All the above images can be seen as being symbols for wisdom, the Logos of Eve.[184]

The waters of these rivers of paradise can be thought of as being a kind of panspermia, a matrix of everything possible,[185] out of which the pneumatics could choose according to their needs. In this way, they were able to achieve knowledge of their own wholeness, of the complete man, by which they mean the inner, spiritual man. According to Jung, "[these images] represent an integration process that is characteristic of psychological individuation."[186]

Thus, the four rivers of paradise in the four corners of the Creation Tapestry refer to the individuation of man, to his gradual achievement of wholeness throughout the course of his life.

In the border at the top of the Tapestry, Annus, the divine personification of the year, sits upon his throne surrounded by the four seasons. Depicted in the borders on the right and left of the Tapestry are the individual months of the year with men working in the open fields. Annus is the image that dominates the borders, which represent everyday life, and this fact draws attention to man's dependence upon time. Medieval man, regardless of his social standing, lived according to cycles and rhythms. This is still essentially true of modern man, even though he is hardly aware of it. Our bodies function according to the rhythm of our blood circulation and breathing. Our days revolve around the cycle of eating, digesting, sleeping, and being awake. In addition, birth and death, health and sickness accompany us throughout life. Because of high birthrates, high rates of mortality amongst children, epidemics and famine, medieval man was more immediately connected to the great, eternal cycles of life. This cycle repeated itself every year. Nature's awakening in spring was followed by the heat of summer, which gave way to autumn's maturity, followed by winter's completion of the cycle. Although medieval man experienced this annual rotation as being God-given, nevertheless he felt himself to be a part of

---

[183] Von Franz, *Passion of Perpetua*, 37.
[184] Ibid., 32.
[185] Jung, *Aion*, vol. 9/II, *CW*, § 312.
[186] Ibid.

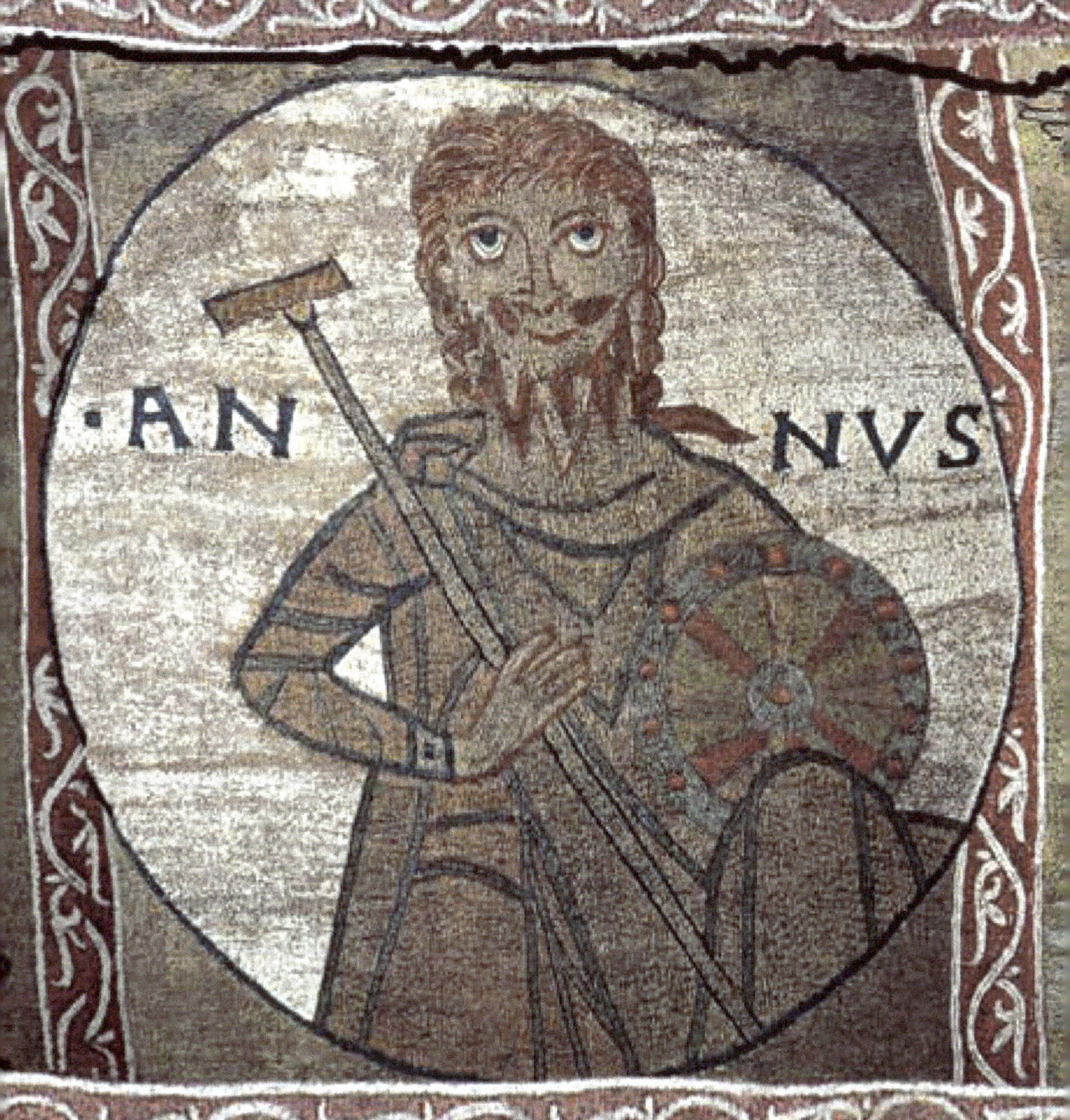

it and therefore he felt he carried some responsibility for it as well. His ever-repeating work and rituals, which he saw as his own obligation, helped him to uphold the natural course of events.

His daily food was dependent upon his seasonal duties: tilling and sowing the fields in spring, harvesting hay and corn in the summer, hunting and butchering in autumn, wood-chopping and looking after his home in the winter. This repetitive work was not only necessary but also was the means by which medieval man felt connected to the rhythm of nature. He was nature's companion, thereby assisting it in its constant cycle of birth, death, and rebirth and supporting it by performing certain rituals. For medieval man, the largest unit of time was one's own life-span, which, at the time, was usually over for both men and women by the sixth decade. A year, on the other hand, was of the same duration for everyone. The year, as such, dominated everyday life, and by counting its repetitions, longer time intervals could be measured. This is why Annus, the Roman personification of the year, is presented as an overly large figure enthroned in the middle of the upper edge of the Creation Tapestry. Cradled in his left arm is the wheel of time which is meant as a symbol of renewal. In his right hand he holds a tool to indicate the creative and progressive aspect of time, for a year is not just an ever-repeating rotation of time but also brings about a progression. Thus, the tool represents the future, development and progress. Time is not only a measure of quantity; it also has quality. Both his size and the white circle which encircles him draw attention to the importance of Annus in comparison to the other figures of medieval everyday life, which are depicted around him.

Two heavenly bodies are placed close to Annus, which determine his inner rhythm, namely, the sun and the moon. By means of its position in the sky, the sun determines the seasons of the year, and by means of its rising and setting it dictates our rhythm of day and night. As the forerunner of the sun, throughout the night, the moon divides the year into months and, by symbolising the feminine, is the basis of all fertility. Both of these heavenly bodies are symmetrically placed on the middle axis of the Creation Tapestry, in the sixth square of the borders on each side. When viewed together, the images of the sun, moon, and Annus form a triangle that encompasses the inner circle of creation. Following pagan tradition, both heavenly bodies are riding across the sky in a four, and two-horse drawn chariot respectively, with the sun (DIES SOLIS means the days of the sun) depicted as a man and the moon (DIES LUNES means days of the moon) depicted as a woman, which corresponds to the image of the fourth day of creation within the inner creation circle. In March, the warmth of the sun begins to be felt, and its chariot is ascending the sky. From October onward, its strength is diminishing and night-time becomes threateningly long, and the chariot of the moon is riding

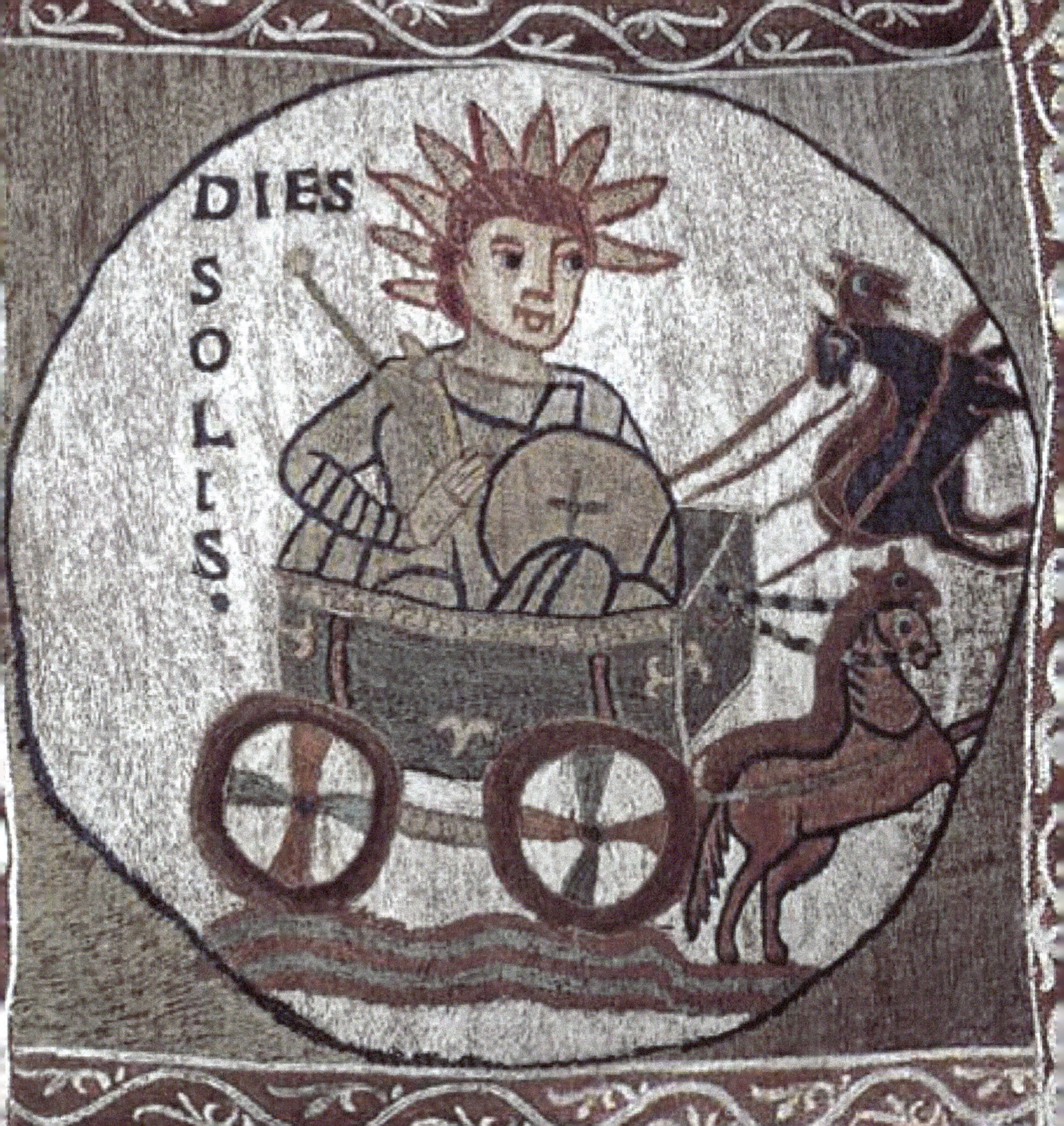

across the sky. Thus, emphasis is given to the male/female double nature of Annus, a fact which our attention has already been drawn to by the tool he holds and the wheel of time which he has with him. The fact that Annus is sometimes depicted as the figure of Christ (as, for example, in the rosette of the western portal of the Gothic cathedral in Lausanne) emphasizes the all-encompassing dimension of God incarnate.

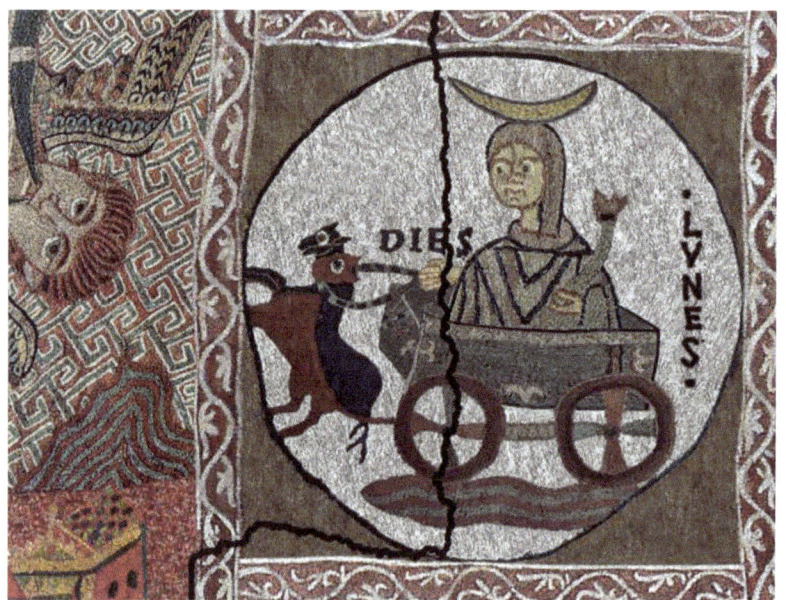

The abbess of the convent of Rupertsberg, Hildegard of Bingen, to whom I have referred above, describes a vision in which she saw the earth as the bearer and carrier of humankind who needs our care. In all its simplicity and beauty, she recognized the earth as being our nature and our home with us bound to it in time. To illustrate her ideas, Hildegard uses representations of the seasons and the months. During the time we are alive, living in space and time as we know it, we experience our own incompatibility with the natural world in which we are less rooted than animals and plants, and we must face the challenge of a painful confrontation with our natural environment. In this regard, a cosmic responsibility has been imposed upon us.

"When God created the nature of man, he also structured the seasons in him. With the summer he gave a hint to the alert active man, with the winter to the sleep. As the winter is hiding in his lap what the summer is putting forth with joy, the sleeping man is strengthened to make him ready with alert powers to implement all kind of work. He discriminated as well the months in man, in so far as He embedded in him the possibilities to differentiate his capabilities and his specific qualities."[187]

---

[187] Hildegard of Bingen, *Welt und Mensch,* 153. (Translated by Kappes)

Hildegard also compares the passing of a single year with the passing of a man's lifetime: the winter months at the outset consist of a slow, persistent search toward growth and development; the months of spring that follow bear witness to an energetic process of unfolding and blossoming; the months of summer and then autumn bring with them a dynamic maturation followed by a harvesting; and finally, the winter months are a time of retirement, of introverted withdrawal into oneself and a closing-down process. She assigns to each month its own elements and qualities as well as its own body parts, experience of the senses, specific stages in life, various psychic states and psychic developments. In this manner, she emphasises how the passage of a year corresponds to the passage of individuation in man.[188]

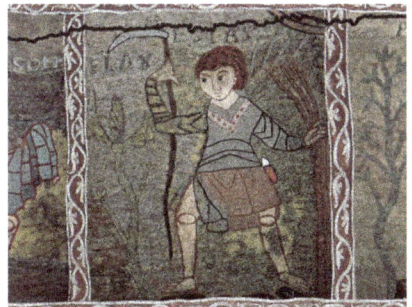

Bearing this in mind, the images depicting the months on the Creation Tapestry are to be understood not simply as depictions of activities that take place throughout a year, but should also be seen as symbolic representations of the passage of individuation in man. The fragmentary image for February of a man collecting things points to the steady accumulation of outer and inner impressions throughout childhood. The image for March is of a man holding a snake and a frog while looking at a stork, all of which point toward fertility and an awakening sexuality. In April, the earth is being tilled, and this refers to preparing the ground for fruitful learning with a view to life as an adult. In May, a horse is being fed, a symbolic representation of the sustenance given to the dominant, creative and powerful life-instinct in the young. In June, a spirited fisherman and birdcatcher symbolizes the active accumulation and translation of inspired ideas and their

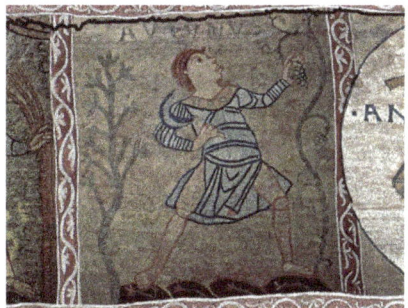

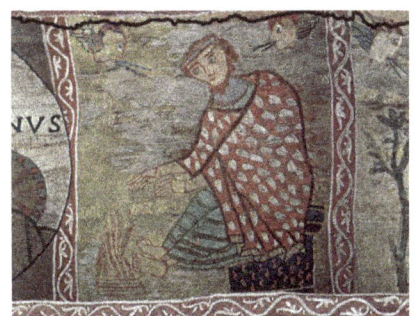

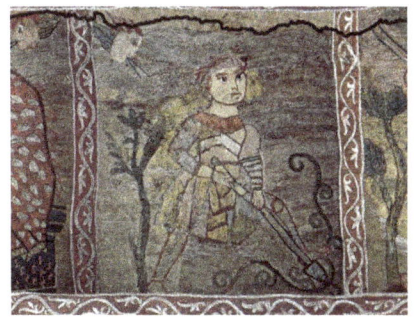

---

[188] Ibid., 153ff.

application in everyday life. These images are followed by the pictures of the year (Annus) and the seasons, the latter being framed by two images from the life of Samson, both of which hint at the problems which arise in mid-life (see page 103/104). In contrast to the aspirations of the first half of life, which are depicted ascending from the lower to the upper left side of the Tapestry, we see the mature second half of life depicted in a descending fashion on the right hand side of the Tapestry. Although the images are only fragmentary, we are still able to recognize in the image of each month that the months from July to October are dealing with illustrations of harvesting: in July, the cutting of the grass; in August, the harvesting of grain; in September, the thrashing of field crops; in October, the picking of grapes. In this way, the harvesting of the second half of life is depicted, beginning with the material and extending to the spiritual (wine). The illustrations for November and December are indecipherable, as is the one for January (see below and page 96).

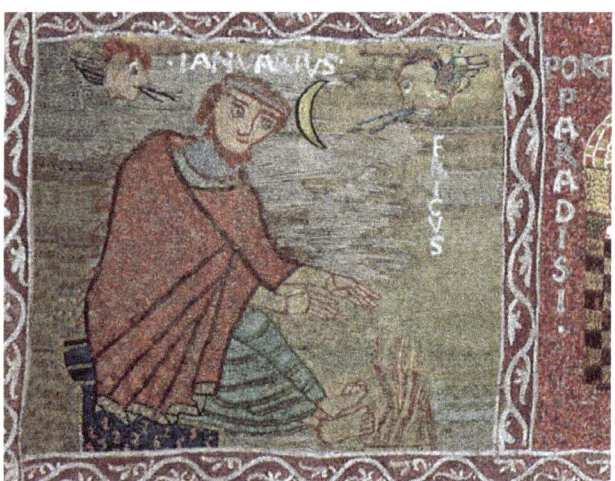 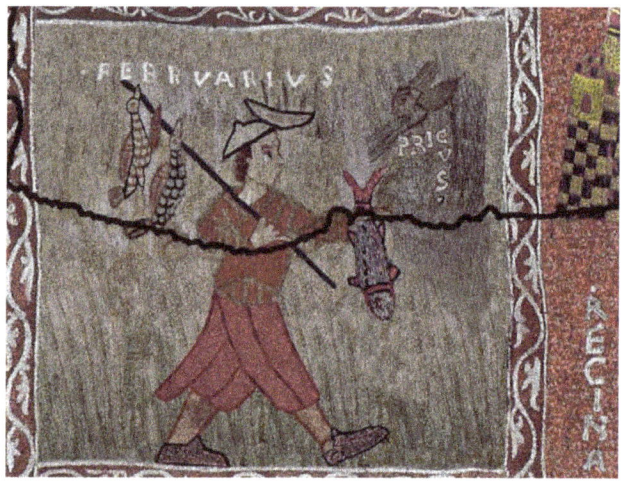

There is an unusual detail in the images of the months, in those that show seasonal work on the land or other activities, which must be mentioned. "Stuck" onto the head of every man is a crescent moon. One has the impression that from February to June a never-changing crescent moon moves across their heads from right to left, or from their foreheads to the back of their heads. It is impossible for us to know if this crescent moon appears in a similar manner in the illustrations of the second half of the year for the Tapestry is so fragmented. It would seem, however, to be probable.

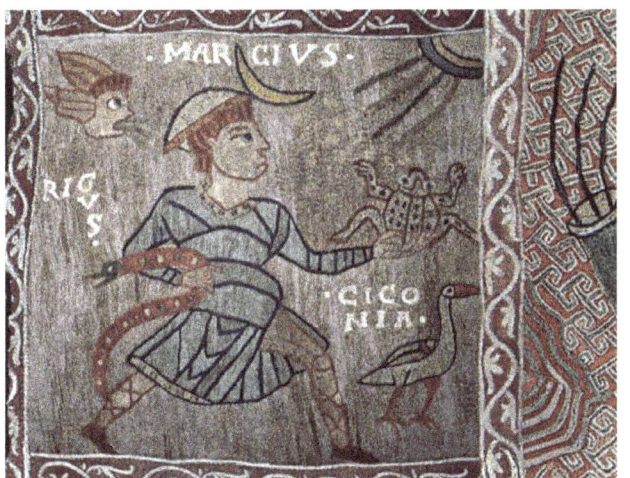 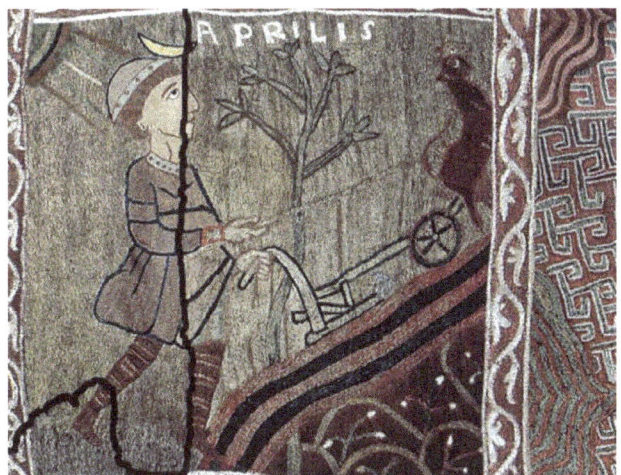

Symbolically speaking, the moon is generally thought of as being a symbol of the feminine, pointing to the maternal qualities of nature which both nurture and pose a challenge for man. Simultaneously, the moon is a symbol of the unconscious. If we pursue Hildegard's train of thought in which the progression of the months is seen as the path of life and individuation, then the changing position of this crescent moon on the heads of the men could point to the feminine way of comprehending life, with the moon being like the Grail cup or vessel of a man in which he carries his most precious treasure, the center of his being, his Self. In the pictures of the first five months, representing childhood and early youth, the moon rests upon the forehead of the men, which is an image of the unconscious which predominates during this phase of life. Before the second half of life begins, that is, in the second quarter of life, the moon moves toward the back of their heads. This points to man's behaviors being increasingly dominated by consciousness. But from mid-life onward, the unconscious regains the upper hand over consciousness and increasingly wants to become integrated into consciousness. In the illustrations of the second half of the year, and of life, perhaps the moon gradually moves back again to the foreground, that is, onto their foreheads. This about-face in mid-life brings hidden dangers with it as the images from the legend of Samson indicate (see page 98 and 100).

Embedded within the framework of this symbolical way of viewing things, the images of the sun and moon chariots fit in well with the illustrations of the months. At the time of childhood and youth, the sun chariot

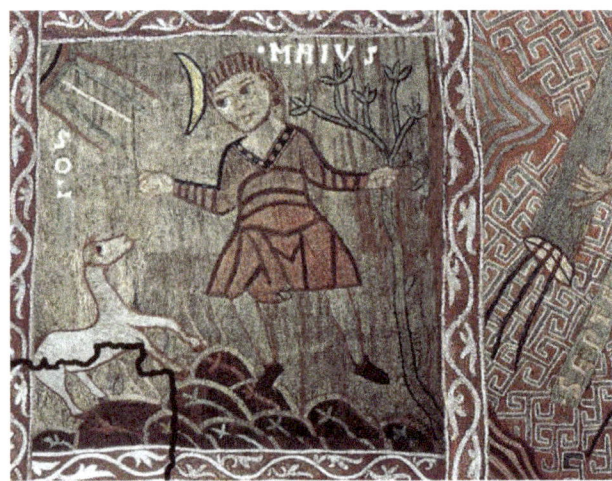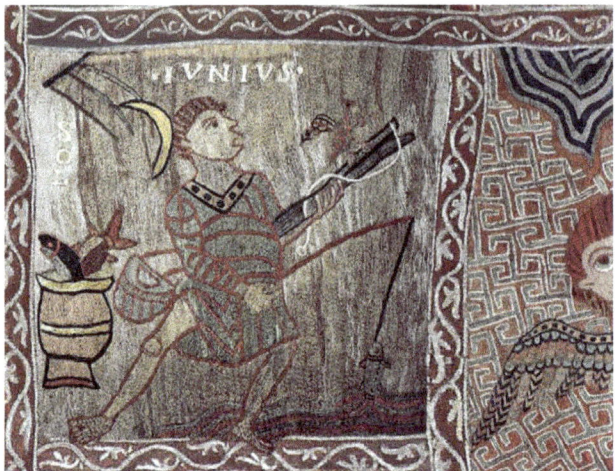

is depicted ascending, that is, the light of consciousness dominates this stage of life. In old age, the moon chariot is ascending, that is, the unconscious must be given growing attention. In the course of a lifetime, it is the unconscious with its basic feminine qualities that dominates at both the beginning and the end. In the middle years of one's life, however, it is the bright light of consciousness with its male, rational qualities that outshines the unconscious.

In Sufism, the moon symbolises the "universal prototype," Mohammed or Adam, who is the mirror in which the light of the world is reflected. This light, however, represents the manifestation of divine understanding. Translated into the world of the mystic, this means that his soul becomes the image of the moon, which reflects the divine light. It is the spiritually divine inspiration of a mystic about the true nature of God.[189] The moon crescent in particular is used to symbolise the mystic's ability to receive divine grace. For his soul "sitting upon fire, consumed by light and knowledge, […] is transformed into the full moon which then, as the station cools and contracts, becomes a crescent."[190]

Thus, the frame of the Creation Tapestry expresses a time-bound process through the images of the months and this, in turn, relates to the developmental process of an individual, as well as to the development of the

[189] Bakhtiar, *Sufi*, 59.
[190] Ibid., 89.

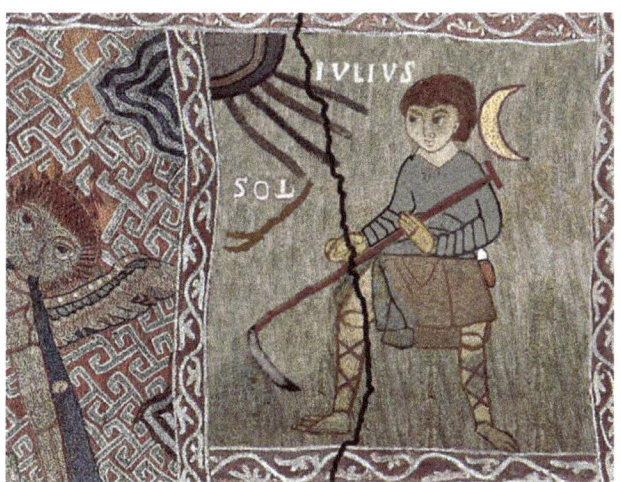 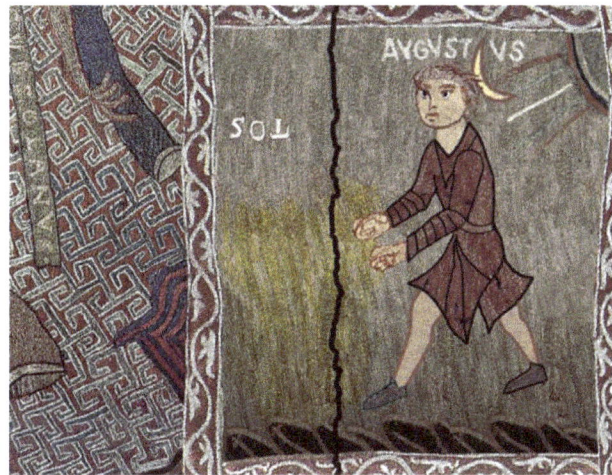

collective, as they unfold through time. In addition, this framework points toward the creative and limiting aspect of time, which an individual may experience within his individuation process. For these reasons, Annus holds not only the wheel of time but also a tool, which implies the creative aspect of time.

The very fact that only men are to be seen in the illustrations of everyday reality in the Creation Tapestry can be understood to indicate that men, in this case, represent *all of humankind*. The Tapestry as a whole, however, reflects the male/female aspect of God and indeed, emphasizes the female aspect of the divine by its form as a mandala, in the image of the dove and its depiction of the legend of St. Helena.

In both the segments in which Adam is depicted in the inner circle, as well as in the sequence of pictures that form the border of the Tapestry (the months, seasons, and so on), the two colors of brown and green, that is, of nature, predominate. Both of these colors are natural life colors. Our earth is brown, as is the humus which covers it, as well as wood and, indeed, feces. On this organic bed, vegetation thrives in every conceivable shade of green. Green stands for the hope of life renewing itself in spring. In both pictures where Adam is portrayed, the creation of new life is depicted, and here, too, natural colors predominate.

It is appropriate that both the geometric calligraphy between the circle of creation and the border images of everyday life, as well as the surrounds of the images of the months, have a red background, for here we are dealing with life being realized in all its painful and joyful aspects.

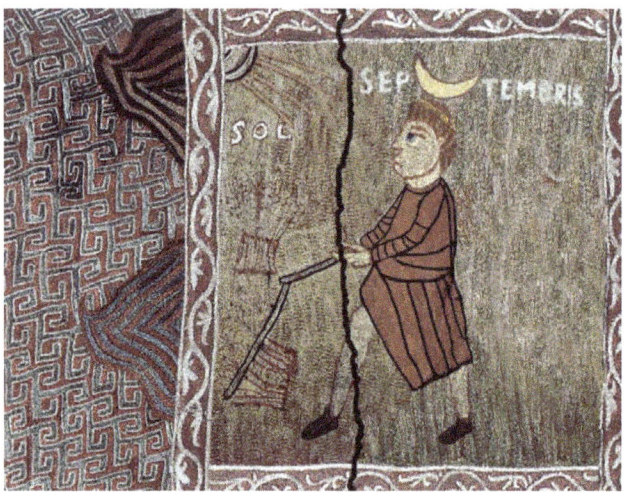

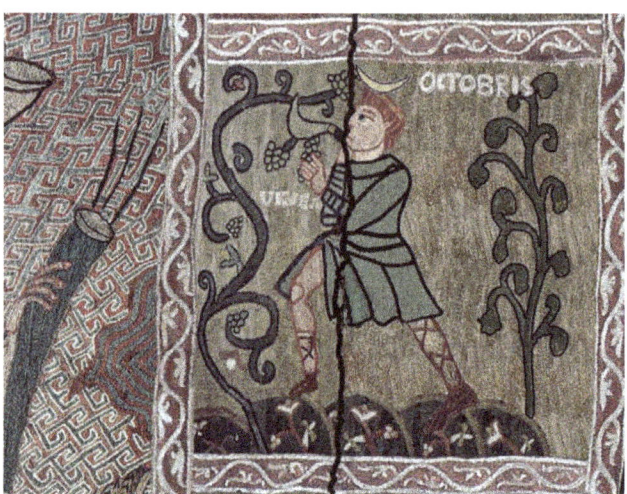

With its images of the months and the seasons, the border of the Creation Tapestry depicts those aspects of the divine which have been realized in space and time, in matter and in the psyche, that is, the concrete aspect of the *unus mundus*. This reality, too, is part of the divine and is, indeed, that side of the divine which we can perceive through sensory experience.

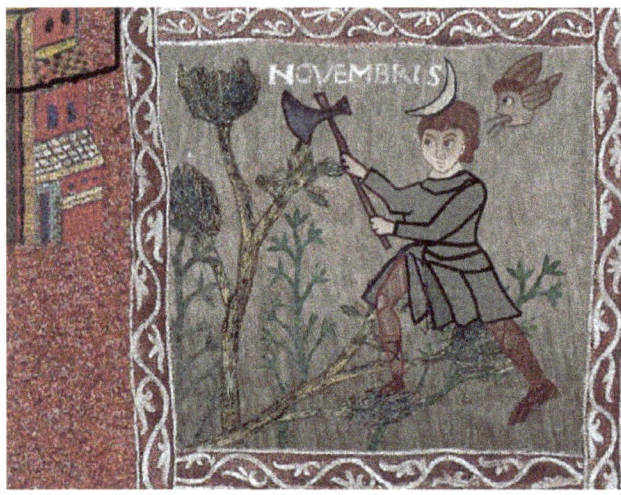

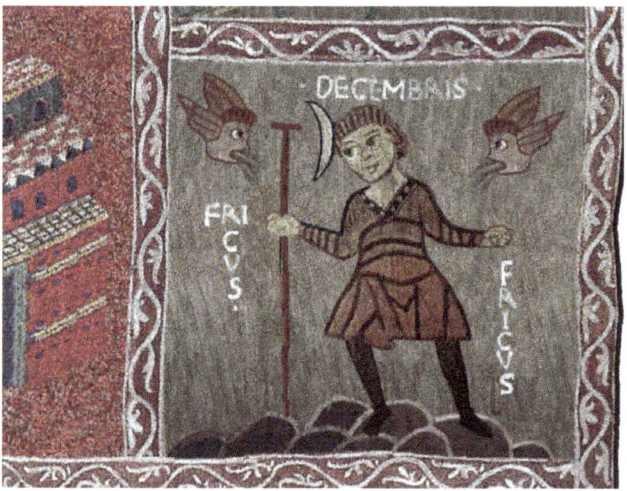

On the upper border of the Creation Tapestry we find two pictures which frame the images of the seasons, and both pictures portray scenes from the life of Samson (vulgata: Samson). The picture on the left-hand side shows a man of superhuman strength swinging the jawbone of an ass. His uncut hair, which gives him divine strength, covers his neck and reaches down to his shoulders. In the upper right-hand corner of this picture stitched in blue thread and thus barely legible is the word "Samson." Whatever he is carrying under the cloth that covers his left arm remains hidden to our view.

In the picture on the right-hand side, Samson is clasping the corpse of a young lion that he has killed with his bare hands while on his way to his bride. In his right hand he is holding a knife, though in a much less powerful way than in the left-hand picture with the jawbone, with which he plans to cut honeycombs out of the lion's carcass. In this picture, too, both strength and courage are portrayed but in a less goal-oriented manner than in the left-hand picture.[191]

The destruction of Samson, of how he tears down the temple, killing himself along with 3,000 Philistines, is depicted on the head or capital of an inner column on the east side of the Romanesque cloisters of the Cathedral of Gerona. Thus, we find the conclusion to the legend of Samson, which was begun with the two pictures in the Creation Tapestry, outside in the cloisters of the Cathedral.

The Legend of Samson

Samson was born to a couple who had long been without any children at a time when the Philistines ruled the land of Israel. An angel had heralded his birth and told his parents not to cut his hair for he was one of God's chosen ones. They were told he would have supernatural strength for he had been chosen to prepare Israel for its freedom from being ruled by the Philistines.

As a youth, Samson fell in love with the daughter of a Philistine and insisted that his parents arrange for him to be married to her. On his way to his bride-to-be, Samson came face-to-face with a young lion who

---

[191] Cf. fn 14: The coloring of the fur, the paws and the tail speak in favor of it being a young lion. In Palol's view, the images of Samson make no sense within the context of the Tapestry (pd).

roared at him. He ripped the lion to pieces with his bare hands. *Some time later while on the way to his wedding, he again passed this way and saw the carcass of the lion in which a swarm of bees had built its nest. He cut out some of the honeycomb and gave some of it to his parents to eat.*[192]

Although they were afraid of him, 30 companions of his bride had been invited to their wedding feast which went on for seven days. He asked them to solve this riddle:

"Out of the eater came forth food,
And out of the strong came forth sweetness."

When three days passed without their having solved the riddle, the bride's companions persuaded her to make Samson reveal the solution. For the rest of their wedding feast, Samson's bride cried on his shoulder

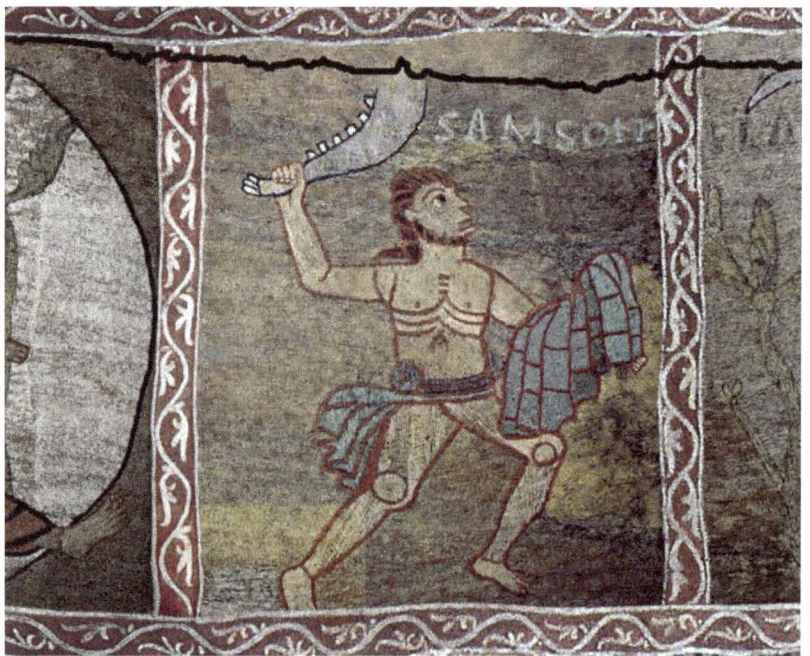

until finally, he told her of his encounter with the lion and his removal of the honey. His wife told the riddle to her companions, and so it came about that Samson lost his bet. Because he had promised each one of her companions a linen garment as their prize for solving the riddle, Samson went out and killed thirty men in a nearby town and stripped them of their garments. Because of her role in this incident, Samson left his wife in great anger and returned to live in his parent's house.

---

[192] This scene is depicted in the upper frame on the outer right side of the picture (in front of the River in the Garden of Eden).

Some time later, he wanted to go back to his wife. Her father, however, would not let him enter her chamber for, in the meantime, he had given his daughter to Samson's companion. Enraged, Samson took revenge by setting the grain fields of the Philistines on fire by tying firebrands onto the tails of three hundred foxes. As a result, the Philistines burnt down his father-in-law's house, destroying his family and his belongings.

These events aroused anger among the men of Judah for they feared the wrath of the Philistines who ruled over them, and so they wanted to bind Samson and deliver him into the hands of their enemies. Agreeing to their plan, Samson allowed himself to be bound and taken before the Philistines. But once there, he tore the ropes which bound him and smote a thousand Philistines with the jawbone of an ass.[193]

When Samson went to visit a prostitute, the Philistines lay in wait for him at the city gates, locking them well at night so that he could not escape. When Samson went to leave the city after midnight, he unhinged the gates and, to mock his enemies, he carried them to the top of a nearby mountain.

Samson fell in love with Delilah some time later, and the Philistines prevailed upon her to find out wherein Samson's superhuman strength lay. Thrice Samson was able to stall her questions with a lie, but on the fourth occasion, convinced of her love for him, he confided in her and disclosed his divine secret that his strength lay in his hair, which had never been cut. He then fell asleep with his head resting in her lap. She shaved his head and sent for the Philistines who easily overpowered him, blinded him and forced him to do the work of a slave. During a sacrificial feast to thank their God, Dagon, for delivering the great Samson into their hands, they sent for Samson to appear before them in order to mock the blind and defenceless man. But by this time, Samson's hair had grown back a little, and his strength had partly returned and by leaning upon them, he was able to pull down the two main columns of the palace, burying 3,000 Philistines along with himself. His family later found and buried him with all due honor in the tomb of his father.[194]

---

[193] This scene is depicted in the upper frame on the outer left side of the picture (beside the River Geon in the Garden of Eden).
[194] Judg. 13–17.

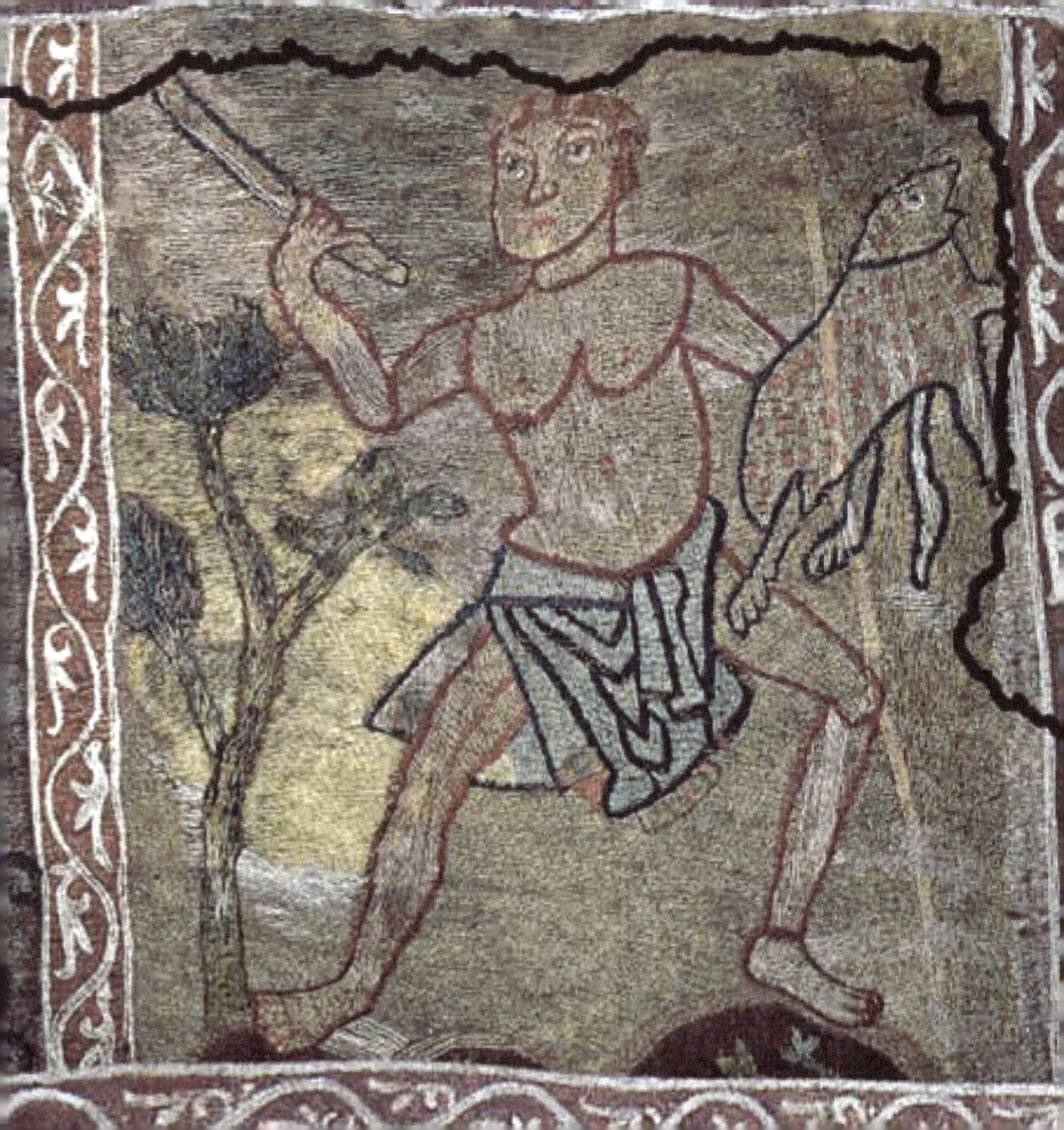

It is quite possible that the myth of Samson is a collection of several different myths, for instance, the myth of Hercules, to which it bears a strong resemblance. The name "Samson" means "small sun" or "man of the sun" in Hebrew. This points to a connection, perhaps also an etymological connection, to "Simon," "Semo," "Sem," which is the name of a god and is derived from "Shemesh," which means "Sun God." Jung believed that the myth of Samson was undoubtedly related to the Shemesh myth, the myth of Baal.[195] Just as the strength of the sun is in its rays, so too was Samson's divine strength in his hair. Moreover, the fact that he was brought into the world by a couple who had been infertile up to that time is an indication of his being a divine incarnation.

The zodiacal sign which rules over the most intense heat of the summer is the lion.[196] He is a sun animal, with his impressive mane resembling the rays of the sun. Louis XIV was born under the zodiacal sign of the lion and went down in history as "le roi soleil."[197] When Samson killed the lion, he killed himself for, like Hercules, he fought with his bare hands because he was fighting against himself. In the blazing sun of July and August, everything the sun had previously nurtured would seem to be burnt up by its heat. By sacrificing its own creations, the sun brings on the ripeness of autumn at the end of the summer season. But the fruits of autumn carry within themselves the seed of rebirth for the following spring.[198] This self-sacrificing aspect of the sun is reflected in Samson's overpowering of the lion and his harvesting of the honey from the lion's carcass. In the same vein, Samson's act of setting the Philistine's grain fields on fire is a further symbolic depiction of the scorching blaze of the summer's sun. Thus, self-sacrifice can be seen as a preparation for rebirth. The hero of a Mithraic myth also does battle with a bull and kills him.[199] And from this death all fertility grows. This same symbolic transformation from death to rebirth is an intrinsic part of Christian communion. The body and blood of Christ are transformed into bread and wine, which we partake of in the belief that by doing so we will be transformed through spiritual rebirth.

---

[195] Jung, *Symbols of Transformation*, vol. 5, *CW*, § 460: see fn 70.
[196] Ibid., § 425.
[197] Riemann, *Astrologie*, 107.
[198] Jung, *Symbols of Transformation*, vol. 5, *CW*, § 553.
[199] Cumont, *Mysterien des Mithra*.

Thus, the image of "Annus" together with both pictures from the legend of Samson, as well as the images of the seasons, which they frame, represent the cycle of time in the here and now with its continual transformation of death into rebirth through self-sacrifice. Samson's riddle also emphasises the mystery behind the cyclical rhythm of vegetation:

"Out of the eater came forth food,
and out of the strong came forth sweetness."

In the Middle Ages, the passing of time was above all experienced as a cycle in which man performed his duties according to the ever-recurring cyclical transformations. Indeed, medieval man felt that by performing his duties in accordance with the season, he was not only supporting the cycle of the seasons, but was, in fact, causing it to happen. In this way, medieval man was conscious of his personal responsibility for cosmic transformation for according to his view, by being a part of nature himself, both his labor and his rituals contributed to upholding the annual cycle of nature. He, too, was responsible for the eternal dance of summer to autumn, of winter to spring, a dance of vigorous intensity bearing a rich harvest, and of quiet withdrawal bringing re-awakened hope.

The individual lived his life according to this rhythmic expansion and contraction of the seasonal year and was subjected to its unshakeable laws. The first half of life was one of vigorous expansion, of intense living and rich harvesting, while the second half was one of contraction, of quiet introversion and, ultimately, death and resurrection in the Kingdom of God. This transition from the first to the second half of life involves self-sacrifice for, unexpectedly, both the principle of logos in men and the principle of eros in women turn against them in order to enforce a change of personality. In men, this new challenge is symbolically represented by the feminine, a sister/mother/wife figure, a demonic woman who threatens him, or rather, his logos principle.[200]

In the legend of Samson, it is Delilah, to whom he entrusts his secret and who betrays him and thus strips him of his divine powers, who is the agent of this new challenge. By cutting his hair, the Philistines are able

---

[200] Jung, *Symbols of Transformation*, vol. 5, *CW*, § 458.

to capture Samson, to blind him and force him into slavery. He sinks into eternal night, that is, he is overwhelmed by the unconscious. As an individual, his task would be to integrate the unconscious into consciousness, to balance what he is conscious of with what he is not conscious of within the framework of his individuation process and thus keep his psychic energy available for transformation. Samson does not succeed in doing this and he becomes a blind slave who cannot live according to his own free will but rather must live according to the will of others. In psychological terms, this means that he is now driven by complexes, or shadow-sides of his personality. On a personal level, this corresponds to a man who, because he is unable to integrate his devouring mother complex into consciousness and thereby neutralize it, is caught by his complex, both in his behavior as well as in his psychological development, with the result that in both areas he becomes paralyzed and blocked. Accordingly, the two images of Samson in the Creation Tapestry emphatically warn of how dangerous it is for a man to adopt a purely masculine attitude toward life, and further, they warn of the danger of having a correspondingly purely masculine image of God whose feminine side has been either forgotten or repressed.

During his lifetime, Samson repeatedly becomes entangled in feeling problems that he fails to solve and which then prompt him each time to take brutal revenge. Indeed, it is his weak feeling-side that finally costs him his heroic life. With his superhuman strength, he is repeatedly the victor where masculine strength is the determinant of a fight. He never shuns a fight and indeed, even looks for it. But his final defeat is brought about because he falls in love with women who betray him. His purely masculine, courageous, forward-looking attitude runs counter to his naive trust in his lovers. Here, too, we are confronted with a one-sided attitude that over-emphasizes the masculine and does not form a mature relationship to the feminine foundation of his soul and which therefore perishes. In Hebrew, Delilah means "little whore."

The reason for Samson's downfall can be found in his weak feeling-function. Such men, even today, can appear at first glance to be utterly charming, related and fine-feeling types in their relationships to women. This is possible if, as a child, such a man has adopted the anima of his warm-hearted father instead of the cold and removed attitude of his mother complex. But such a man is incapable of deeper relationships and attachments. Honest and deep feelings and relatedness remain unknown to him. Thus, the two images of Samson in the Creation Tapestry can be said to represent a life with too little depth of feeling and relatedness, and such a life finds its reflection in a purely masculine God image. This problem becomes particularly acute in the second half of a man's life, which explains why the Samson images are placed between June and July; these two months represent the middle of the year, or symbolically, the middle of life when it is essential for a man to overcome his "Samson complex." This task is the precondition for the continuation of his individuation process in the second half of his life.

It seems obvious that these two pictures from the legend of Samson represent a collective insight, which recognized that an open, heroic confrontation with Islam and Judaism could not, ultimately, lead to any change in the threatening situation of that time other than, perhaps, the loss of thousands of lives. A purely masculine attitude toward believers of different faiths needed to be sacrificed, for such an attitude would have had fatal consequences. A more feeling-related attitude, with an inner relationship to both the divine (which includes both the masculine and feminine aspects of its totality) and to human wholeness (which includes both the unconscious as well as conscious aspects of its totality) would lead to a more successful meeting of the very different, but very invigorating, beliefs of both Islam and Judaism. Of what possible benefit could Samson's slaying of a thousand Philistines be to the Israelites? Without any regard for unconscious contents or without any connection to the feminine side of a man's soul, such a courageous act remains a mere display of strength. In this respect, the legend of Samson teaches the Christians how dangerous it is for them to try to ensure their own existence in relation to non-believers by adopting this purely masculine approach. Rather, an attitude which recognized and took seriously the feminine side of their God, as well as striving to become conscious of the feminine contents of their own soul, could strengthen Christianity in its struggle for autonomy.

In this respect, the Muslims and Jews of this time were no further advanced than the Christians, for Allah and Jahweh are also emphatically masculine Gods, whose feminine aspect is split off. Sufism, however, was noticeably more well-disposed toward women; for example, from early on, women were permitted to attend gatherings of Sufi-preachers.[201] In Arabic and Persian texts of the 9th and 10th centuries, mention is made of

---

[201] Schimmel, *Mystical Dimensions of Islam*, 427.

a considerable number of women because of their remarkable achievements in piety and in asceticism.[202] Sufis were well aware of the positive side of the feminine and in Islam, in which Mohammed's youngest daughter, Fatima (who died in 633) is venerated, Eve was never blamed for the fall of Adam.[203] Above all, the Sufis loved Maria, Maryam, who remained immaculate despite giving birth to the holy child, Jesus. Even today, they worship at the alleged site of her tomb in Ephesos.[204] Two saintly women, one of which was Fatima of Cordoba, were mystical guides and teachers to one of Islam's greatest thinkers, Ibn 'Arabi. It was said of Fatima, "who, in spite of her great age of 95 years, was beautiful and fresh like a young girl, completely transformed by divine love."[205] These encounters may form the basis of Ibn 'Arabi's idea of regarding the feminine as being the true manifestation of God's mercy and of His creative power.[206]

In this respect, medieval minstrels and the Sufis had something in common: the solution to their problem lay hidden in becoming conscious of, and integrating, their own feminine side, and in recognizing the feminine aspects of God.[207]

Judaism was confronted with a similar problem. In the second half of the 13th century (about 150 years after the making of the Creation Tapestry), a secret, new Jewish doctrine, the Kabbala, was developed, which, for centuries to come, was to have a lasting influence on Judaism. One chapter of the Kabbala, the Book of Sohar, presents its own new version of Yahweh's creation story. Like Allah, Yahweh too, was a passionate, angry, masculine God whose feminine aspect, His Schechina, had become increasingly insignificant and meaningless from the early days of Judaism onward. Only in the "Book of Sohar" in the Kabbala was the importance of Yahweh's feminine aspect emphasized.[208]

---

[202] Ibid.

[203] Ibid., 429.

[204] Ibid.

[205] Ibid., 430.

[206] Ibid., 430–31.

[207] Generally speaking, sexuality is not repressed in Islam, but beyond this, there is seldom a deeply personal relationship between a man and a woman. Within Christianity, suffering is required for there to be a personal relationship, which means that the sexual problem often remains unresolved. Cf. Jung and von Franz, *The Grail Legend*, 232.

[208] This masculine God-image is still mirrored in patriarchal Jewish society today, as well as, for example, in the concepts of modern Jews such as Karl Marx's communist teachings, or the psychological theories of Sigmund Freud and Alfred Adler.

In its endeavor to integrate the feminine aspect of a masculine God-image, and to make the feminine aspect of God conscious, Sufism was ahead of Christianity.[209] But in the choice of images used in the Creation Tapestry and in its form as a mandala, the Creation Tapestry reflects a new and more comprehensive image of God, which compensated the collective Christian conscious attitude at the time. However, this new way of thinking about God with its urgently needed regard for the feminine, which had come out of the unconscious, later suffered repeated setbacks. But there is much evidence that, at the close of the 20th century, we are experiencing essentially the same constellation of recognizing the importance of the feminine aspect of God. The future will reveal whether or not our culture will succeed this time around—or whether we will perish.[210]

---

[209] Schimmel, *Mystical Dimensions of Islam*, especially the chapter: "The feminine Element in Sufism," 426.
[210] Jung, *Aion*, vol. 9/II, *CW.*

THE LEGEND OF THE HOLY CROSS

It is quite likely that almost one third of the surface area of the original undamaged Creation Tapestry had a background of wine-red stitching with sequential images depicting the legend of the Finding of the Holy Cross by St. Helena in the foreground. Or perhaps the images portrayed the whole story of the Legend of the Cross, of which its finding by St. Helena is only the final part. On the lower, ragged edge of the Creation Tapestry, both the cross in the center and the jewelled crown beside it are images which relate to a statue of Constantine the Great, where he is holding a cross in his arms.[211] Legend has it that Constantine the Great conquered Maxentius, the heathen emperor of the Western Roman Empire, on the Milvian bridge. On the night before the battle took place, it is said that Constantine had a dream in which a voice drew his attention to a shining cross in the sky and the voice announced: "This is the sign which will lead you to victory."

Whereupon, Constantine gave the order to have the Christian cross painted on the shields of his soldiers. At a later date, he declared Christianity to be the religion recognized by Rome. It was only shortly before his own death, however, that he allowed himself to be baptized.

On the Finding of the Holy Tree[212]

When Adam, the father of all mankind, was about to die, his son, Seth, was in such great distress that he ran back to the gate of paradise and cried out loudly to God, asking Him for His help. So God sent Archangel

---

[211] Palol, "Une broderie catalane," 44–45.
[212] Jacobus de Voragine, *Golden Legend*, 269–76.

Michael to Seth, and the angel gave him a branch from the tree of knowledge of good and evil, and the angel told Seth that he should plant this branch in the earth and as soon as it bears the fruit it is preordained to bear, the curse of sin and death will be lifted from mankind.

Taking the branch with him, Seth returned to his father but his father had died in his absence. Trusting in the wisdom of almighty God, Seth planted the branch near the summit of Mount Lebanon, and he buried his father at the same place. The branch grew into a tree which was taller and stronger than the other trees on the mountainside.

Later, King Solomon sent his carpenters to build a splendid temple in the city of Jerusalem. They came to Mount Lebanon and found the tree which Seth had planted and they chopped it down, along with other trees, and took them all to the city of Jerusalem. The carpenters noticed that the trunk of Seth's tree did not match to the other trees, so they put it aside. When King Solomon saw the tree trunk lying unused, he ordered his men to take it to the Valley of Kidron and to use it to construct a bridge over the brook which flowed through the Valley.

Some time later, a very wealthy queen from the land of Sheba, who was wise beyond all measure, came to vie with Solomon for the reputation of having supreme wisdom. She saw that Solomon lived up to his reputation in every way. He showed her the city of Jerusalem and led her down to the Valley of Kidron where they crossed the bridge which was made out of the tree of knowledge. But while on the bridge, the Queen of Sheba suddenly stood still and with great alarm, she knelt down and prayed. After returning to her own country, she wrote to Solomon saying that he should take good care of that tree trunk for there would come a time when it would be made into a cross and a poor son of man would be nailed to it. She wrote that because of the death of this man, the people of Israel would be cursed and the Kingdom of Solomon would be destroyed. Upon reading this, King Solomon was so greatly alarmed that he had the tree trunk removed in the night and taken to a lonely place in the center of the city and there had it buried in a deep pit. He then saw to it that water filled the pit and a small lake formed. Every day, at daybreak, an angel came down from heaven and made the water move. Many sick people were lying around the edge of the lake for it had been discovered that the first sick person to enter the water after it moved at dawn would be healed.

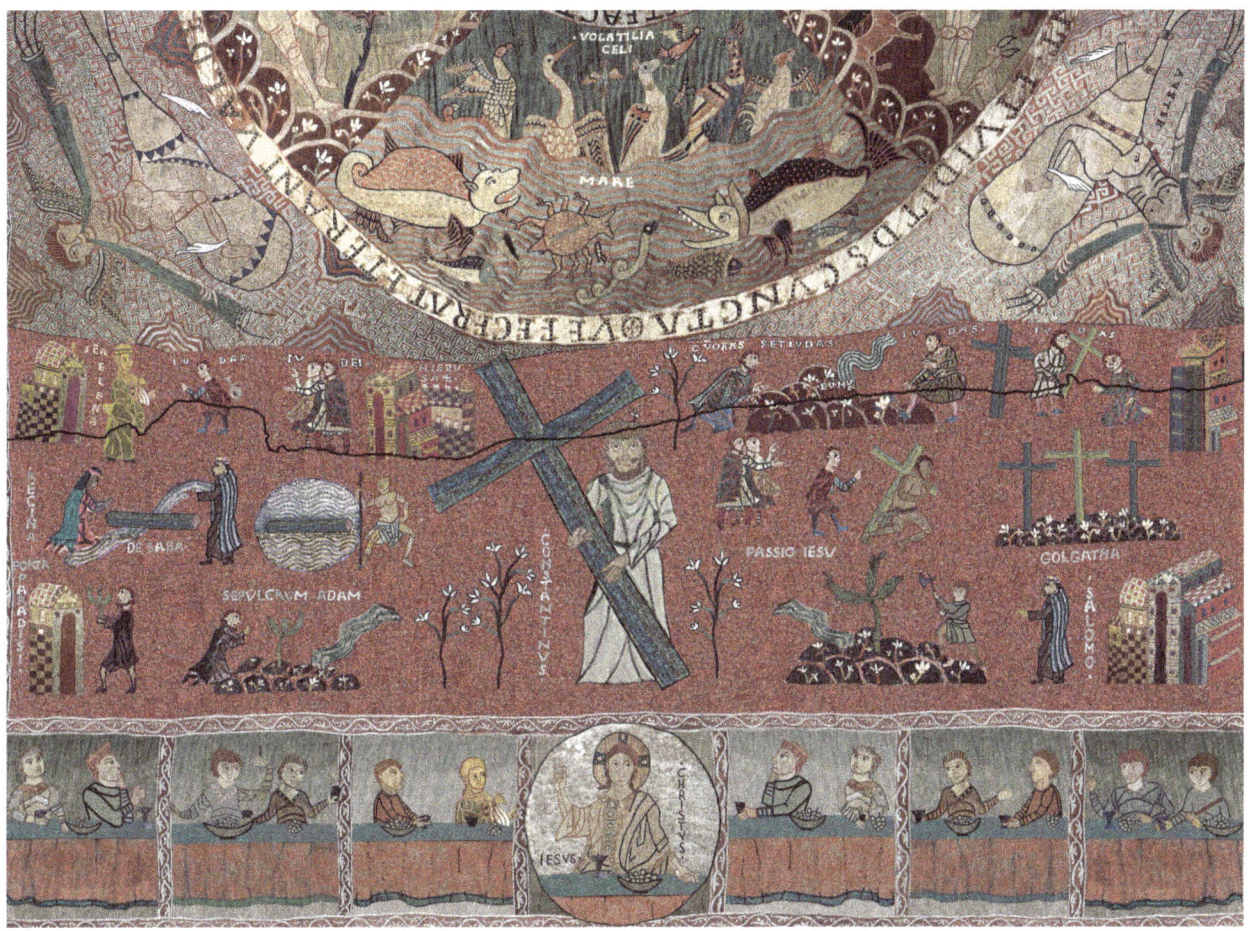

Then followed the years when Jesus Christ walked the earth and was delivered into the hands of his enemies. On the night this happened, the earth shook and the tree trunk which Solomon had hidden rose up to the surface of the lake. And it happened that the carpenters who had been ordered by the High Council to find wood to make a cross for Jesus Christ passed by the lake and in the moonlight saw the floating tree trunk. They pulled it to the shore and made a cross out of it, and it was the cross upon which the Son of God was to suffer and die. After Jesus Christ had risen victoriously from his tomb, the High Council gave orders for the three crosses on which Jesus and the two thieves had died, as well as the instruments of torture used in their crucifixion, to be hidden in a pit on Mount Calvary.

———

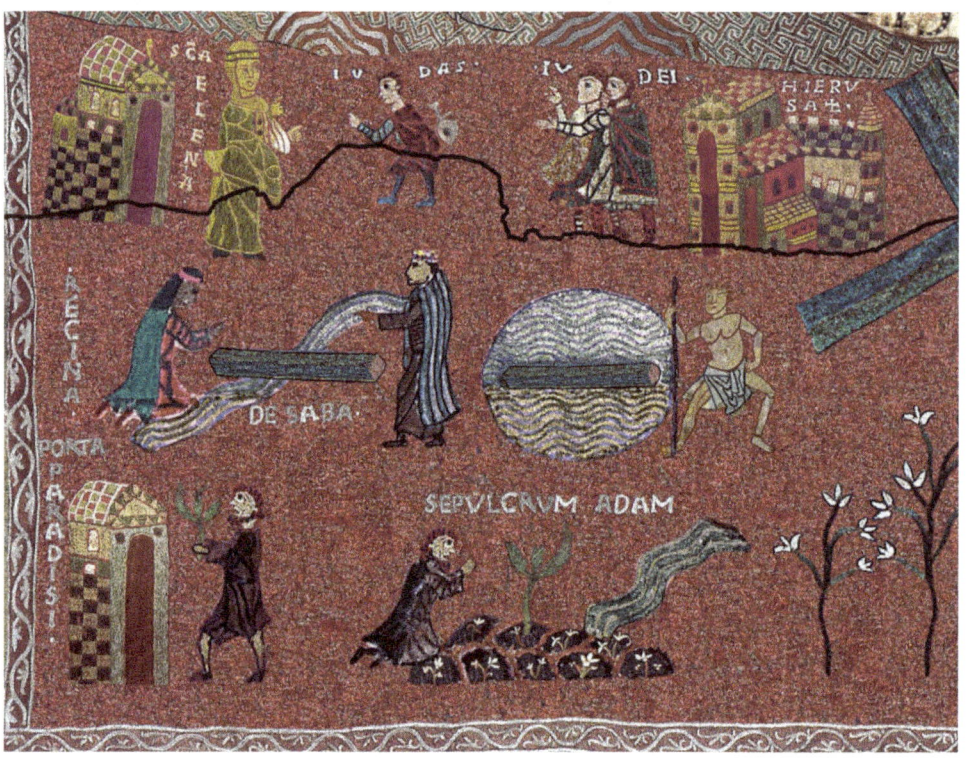

Several hundred years later, Empress Helena came to Jerusalem and called for a meeting with the wise men of the Jewish community. The Jews were struck with fear when they heard that the empress wanted to find out where the cross on which Christ had suffered could be found. Only one person knew of its whereabouts and his name was Judas. He did not want to divulge his secret for his grandfather had told him that when, at some point in the future, people begin to look for the Cross of Christ, the Jewish state will come to an end and those who worship the Crucified One will then rule the land. They took the empress to see Judas for no other Jew was willing to get involved. When the empress put her question to Judas, he replied: "How should I know this, since two hundred years have passed since then, and I was not even born?"[213] Helena asked to be alone with Judas and then said to him: "I swear to thee by the Crucified that I shall let thee die of hunger, if thou refusest to tell me the truth!"[214] And she had him thrown into a dried-out well where he stayed for several days and suffered both hunger and thirst. At last, he asked to be pulled out of the well for he would show the empress where the cross could

---

[213] Ibid., 273.
[214] Ibid., 273–74.

be found. And that is what happened. He led the empress and her retinue to the place, and Helena prayed with great fervour. And suddenly the earth moved, whereupon Judas began to dig vigorously. He uncovered three crosses, but they could not distinguish the Cross of Christ from those of the thieves. So, they took all three crosses and placed them in the center of the holy city, and waited patiently for the Lord to demonstrate his power. And lo, the corpse of a youth was carried past the crosses. Judas brought the procession to a halt and held the first and then the second cross over the dead youth, but the corpse did not move. But when he held the third cross over the corpse, life flowed back into it, and the youth stood up and praised God. This led Judas to become a believer and he was duly baptised and from that time on, he was known as Quivacus. When the Bishop of Jerusalem died, Quivacus was asked to take his place. But Helena took the Cross of Christ to her son, the Emperor Constantine in Constantinople, and it gave her great joy to give it to him.

Only with Adam's guilt did death come into the world. Through his sin at the tree of knowledge, he became conscious of himself and of his limitations and his own transitoriness. And this very realization separated him from the rest of the animal kingdom and made him human. His ego was born. The expulsion of Adam and Eve from the Garden of Eden is impressively depicted on a frieze around the capital of the south-western pier opposite the entrance in the Romanesque cloister of the Cathedral of Girona. There is a Jewish legend which describes what happened to the tree of

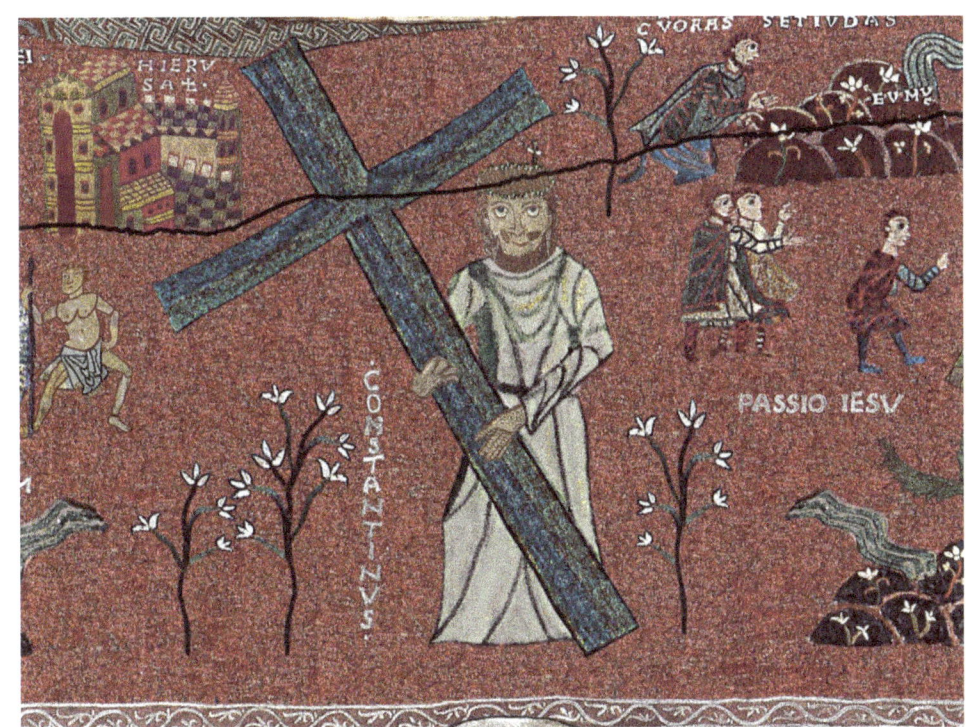

paradise after the Fall of Adam: "Anyone who was allowed to cast a glance into the Garden of Eden after Adam's sin saw the tree of knowledge and the four rivers of paradise. However, the tree of knowledge had withered and in its branches lay an infant. "Mother had become pregnant."[215]

Like water and earth, a tree is a symbol of the mother, of life-giving nature and the unconscious. And in the same manner as the moon, which governs the night, gives birth to the sun, Adam's consciousness rose up out of the unconscious, making him the first human being who was aware of his own self. This tremendous step initially pitched both Adam and Eve into depression, for the consequence of this sin was their expulsion from the Garden of Eden. This meant they were forced to take care of themselves and their family and had to be responsible for their own lives. From that time on, they were compelled to live with the knowledge that their egos were finite and limited and that their deaths were imminent.

The tree of knowledge, however, survived, for the angel gave Seth a branch that had been taken from it and this branch was planted and grew over the grave of Adam on the hill of Golgotha. And it was from the wood of this tree that the Holy Cross was eventually fashioned, upon which the Second Adam, Jesus, was crucified, thereby redeeming us of the Sin of Adam. "Just as death came into the world through Adam, so life came through Christ."[216] Golgotha, or Calvary, means "place of skulls," a name which points to the eternal spirit that has settled over the place since Adam's death; the spirit, that is, of becoming conscious, and from which suffering and death came into the world.

As we have seen, the tree of knowledge became the tree of death for Jesus. Yet, through his redemption and resurrection, the tree once again took on the symbolic meaning of a mother giving new life through rebirth.[217] And the unconscious does, in fact, have both aspects: it brings death and gives life, it redeems and destroys, and without sacrifice, there can be no transformation.

"The cross, or whatever other heavy burden the hero carries, is *himself*, or rather *the* self, his wholeness, which is both God and animal—not merely the empirical man, but the totality of his being, which is rooted

---

[215] Jung, *Symbols of Transformation*, vol. 5, *CW*, § 368.
[216] Rom. 5:11, 12.
[217] Jung, *Symbols of Transformation*, vol. 5, *CW*, § 368.

in his animal nature and reaches out beyond the merely human toward the divine. His wholeness implies a tremendous tension of opposites paradoxically at one with themselves, as in the cross, their most perfect symbol."[218]

Just as the Cross was a part of the tree of life in the Garden of Eden, so too is our wholeness, the totality of the individual, a part of all-embracing nature. In order to be redeemed, the ego has to surrender itself to this greater totality. Only by complying with the Self does the ego become connected with eternal existence, into which it is thus reborn. Through this act, Jesus has shown each Christian the way back to paradise.

At the time of the Old Testament, the Christian idea of death and rebirth as an act of self-sacrifice leading to redemption, was a foreign idea. This path was only revealed much later by the incarnation of God in Jesus. Being a Jew, Samson belonged to the unredeemed ones, in contrast to the Christians who were redeemed through Jesus.

Both of these heroes, Samson and Jesus, were born of a virgin. Both of their births were announced by an angel, and both possessed supernatural abilities. Samson's strength was restricted to physical strength whereas Jesus' strength was a spiritual one. Samson's path ended in a dark abyss, whereas Jesus was reborn *in the father and in the mother*. In the Creation Tapestry, the Jew, Samson, is presented as being somewhat bigger than the other figures from everyday life. He is depicted as wearing only a loin-cloth and, in both pictures, gives the impression of being a wild and earthy character. Thus, Samson is the personification of the divine natural strength within us all.

In this sense, Samson and Jesus represent two poles or opposites; on the one side, natural strength with no relationship to the spirit, and on the other, spirituality without a connection to nature. When Christ is nailed to the Cross which was made from the tree of knowledge, "the tree brings back all that has been lost through Christ's extreme spiritualization, namely the elements of nature. Through its branches and leaves the tree gathers the powers of light and air, and through its roots those of the earth and the water. Christ was suffering

---

[218] Ibid., § 460.

on account of his split and he recovers his perfect life at Easter, when he is buried again in the womb of the virginal mother."[219]

"The symbolic history of Christ's life shows, as the essential teleological tendency, the crucifixion, viz. the union of Christ with the symbol of the tree. It is no longer a matter of an impossible reconciliation of Good and Evil, but of man with his vegetative (unconscious) life. In the case of the Christian symbol the tree however is dead and man upon the Cross is going to die, i.e., the solution of the problem takes place after death. That is as far as Christian truth goes."[220]

When Helena sets out on her journey to find the Holy Cross, she wants to draw attention to this Christian message and to take it seriously again. As a simple woman of the people who became empress, Helena represents the long-neglected and repressed feminine side of the patriarchal, Roman view of the world. This feminine side of the collective soul of the Roman Empire undertook the task of finding the Cross in the 4th century, A.D. As a result, people came to accept as eternal truth the concept of sacrifice being necessary for wholeness and rebirth to bring about redemption in paradise. The fact that an empress finds the Cross could be understood to mean that this message of renewal comes from the collective unconscious. This knowledge, however, had long been viewed with disdain, just as Constantine's mother had been viewed with disdain by her husband, Constancius, because of her lowly origins. In the light of this background, it makes sense that it was her son, the Emperor Constantine, who declared Christianity to be the official religion of Rome. An unconscious feeling-side prepared the way for this change to take place, and the spirit to which it gave birth then recognised and anchored the new religion in collective consciousness. Seen from the opposite angle, the official recognition of Christianity in the Roman Empire would have been an arbitrary act had not the empress found the Holy Cross beforehand. It was she, this feminine side in the unconscious, who smoothed the way for Christianity in the Roman Empire.

---

[219] Jung, *Letters*, vol. 2, 166–67.
[220] Ibid., 167.

The dark red background of the Creation Tapestry upon which the Legend of the Finding of the Holy Cross of Christ is depicted points to the deep suffering that is always a part of self-sacrifice, and we are reminded of the countless martyrs. Simultaneously, however, red is the color of life and points to rebirth in the Kingdom of God. This is why the coffins of popes are lined with dark red cloth. Perhaps the paleolithic custom of burying their dead in pits colored with ochre indicates a similar belief in rebirth in the beyond.

Thus, this part of the Tapestry points toward making suffering conscious, and toward the attitude of enduring life in a world full of opposites. It also draws attention to the principle of Eros, of love, which helps us to suffer the tension of being in the here and now. In the course of a discussion with the theologian, W. Uhsadel, Jung pointed to a replica of a stained glass window from the Church of the Two Monasteries in Königsfelden,[221] which he had installed in his practice. The colorful glass window depicts Jesus on the Cross and Jung made the remark: "You see, this is the crux for us!" And he went on to say that he had recently returned from a trip to India where he had been deeply impressed by the wisdom of the East. But this wisdom, he said, was unable to come to terms with the central problem of human suffering, for it tries to cast off suffering in life. Western rational thought, however, takes the opposite approach: it tries to rid itself of suffering through drug consumption. Suffering, however, said Jung, can neither be gotten rid of, nor can it be subdued. It has to be overcome by being endured. "We learn that only from Him!"[222] Jung concluded.

It is highly probable that Constantine the Great is the figure who is in the center of the Legend of the Holy Cross in the lower part of the Tapestry. Thus, the three most significant figures of the Tapestry are situated on its central axis: Annus at the top; Pantocrator in the middle and Constantine the Great at the bottom, the latter being the symbol which represents the introduction and anchoring of Christianity in the consciousness of the West. This standpoint becomes more meaningful when seen in conjunction with the history of Spain in the late Middle Ages. Around 1100, with Gerona as its center, the Spanish province was cut off from the European Christian world in the north, and to the south it was under cultural, economic, and military threat

---

[221] Canton of Aargau, 14th century.
[222] Uhsadel in Bash et al., *Der unwahrscheinliche Jung*, 133. (Translated by Kappes)

from the successful forces of Islam. By calling the Tapestry, "the Tapestry of Charlemagne about the story of Emperor Constantine" (as it is listed in the protocol for the visit of King Charles V) its creators succeeded in naming the two most successful secular rulers who were engaged in the fight for the spread of Christianity. We can recognize the significance of the Tapestry's name in the light of the threat Gerona was under from Islam over many centuries.

SUGGESTIONS FOR THE MISSING SECTIONS OF THE TAPESTRY

If one restores the missing pictures of the months on the right and left-hand borders of the Tapestry, as well as the centrally symmetric corner pictures of the third and fourth rivers of paradise, the Tapestry once more regains the format of a square which is customary for mandalas, including Christian ones.[223] Nothing can be said with any certainty about the pictures of the three missing months. But, as three of the four pictures of the seasons on the uppermost border are identical with the months to which they correspond, and as, in addition, these pictures are set at regular intervals throughout the year, it seems likely that the picture for the month of January corresponded to the picture of winter. Thus, it probably showed a man warming himself by the side of a fire, though he would have been facing the center of the Tapestry. For the month of November, I arbitrarily chose the image of a man at work in the forest for this month is particularly suited to wood-chopping. Also random was my choice of subject for the month of December which shows a man, leaning on a stick, waiting for spring to arrive. Like the image for January, the December picture also faces the center of the Tapestry.

Inside the border, the lower third of the Tapestry was very likely dedicated to the depiction of the Legend of the Finding of the Holy Cross, together with a description of its origin from the tree of knowledge. This comprehensive legend is so rich in motifs that there is no difficulty to fill in the foreground of the remaining space with scenes which match in size and in density as dictated by the surviving fragments. Set against the

---

[223] Cf. Palol, *El Tapíz de la Creació*, ill. 60 and 61, as well as Calzada, "El mosaic de Beth-Alpha," 200, although in the latter it is wrongly depicted in the image of the sun and moon carriage, cf. also here fn 13.

THE CREATION TAPESTRY OF GIRONA (SPAIN) FROM AROUND 1100

red background, the central figure of the Roman Emperor, Constantine the Great, is as tall as the space he fills permits. His crown, which is richly encrusted with jewels, can still be recognized, as well as the Cross, which he is probably holding at a slight angle.[224] The detailed Legend of the Cross begins where the series of pictures about the cycle of creation stops, that is, with Adam in the Garden of Eden, and it leads us to the finding of the Holy Cross of Christ. Fragments of the Holy Cross were venerated as relics in the Cathedral of Gerona and throughout the Western world and they provide a link to the past.

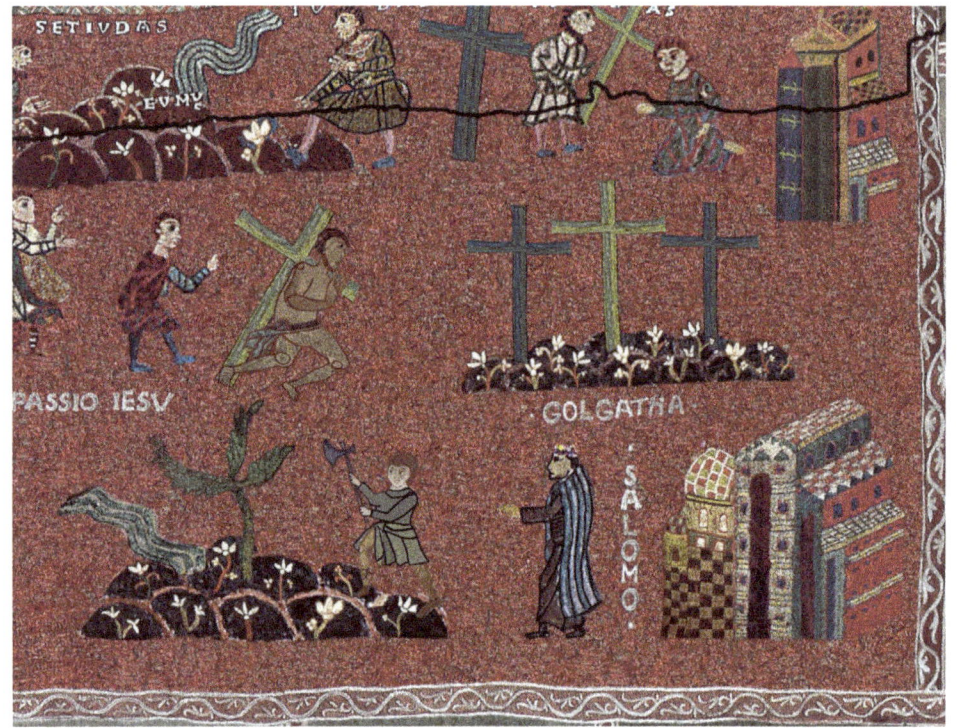

Although the possible choice of scenes from the Legend with which this part of the Tapestry was embellished is un-limited, the available space makes it likely that only the main themes from the Legend were chosen. (From the lower left to the upper right):

Scene 1: Seth, the son of Adam, is given a branch from the tree of knowledge in front of the gates of paradise.

Scene 2: The tree of knowledge grows on top of Adam's grave.

Scene 3: The tree of knowledge is cut down for the construction of King Solomon's temple.

224 Palol, "Une broderie catalane," 244ff.

Scene 4: As the tree is not used in the construction work, King Solomon orders it to be used as a bridge over a river. The Queen of Sheba kneels in prayer by the bridge for she has had a vision in which the true significance of the wood is revealed to her.

Scene 5. The tree is put into a pond and sinks. Thereafter, the water of the pond is believed to have healing powers.

Scene 6: The wood of the tree of knowledge is used to make the Holy Cross, and Jesus carries the Cross up Mount Golgotha.

Scene 7: The three crosses of execution stand on Mount Golgotha.

Scene 8: Saint Helena is told by the Jew, Judas, where the Holy Cross has been buried on Mount Golgotha.

Scene 9: Judas prays, digs, and finds the Cross.

Scene 10: Judas holds the Cross over a kneeling man who is ill. The man is healed and thus the Cross is revealed as being the Cross of Christ.[225]

This list of motifs is only one of the many possibilities which could have completed this section of the Creation Tapestry. In my view it is, however, the most likely choice, though the details leave many questions unanswered.

The most interesting and meaningful question in the reconstruction of the Tapestry concerns the motifs of the seven remaining images along the bottom edge of the Tapestry. For reasons of symmetry, but above all because of the fact that the Creation Tapestry has the form of a Christian mandala, it seems safe to presume that the lower edge was made up of seven square panels, the middle one of which being given particular importance by including a white circle which corresponds to the Annus picture in the center at the upper edge. The largest and most important figures of the Tapestry are positioned along a central axis: Annus at the top, the Pantocrator in the center and Constantine the Great standing in the lower third of the

---

[225] In one variation of the legend, Judas holds the cross of Christ over a corpse that is thereby brought back to life.

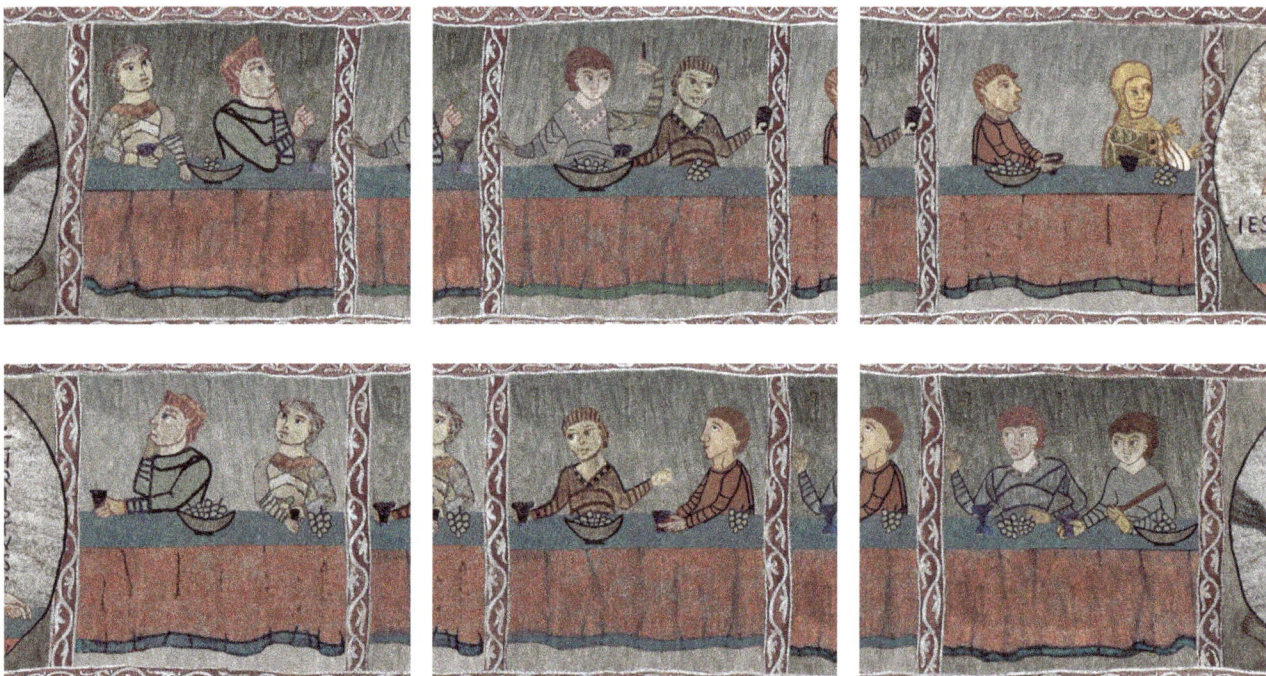

composition.[226] It is my conviction that the most important figure in the center square of the lower edge must be an image of Jesus Christ. As He became incarnate as the Son of God in this world and also died on the Cross as our re-

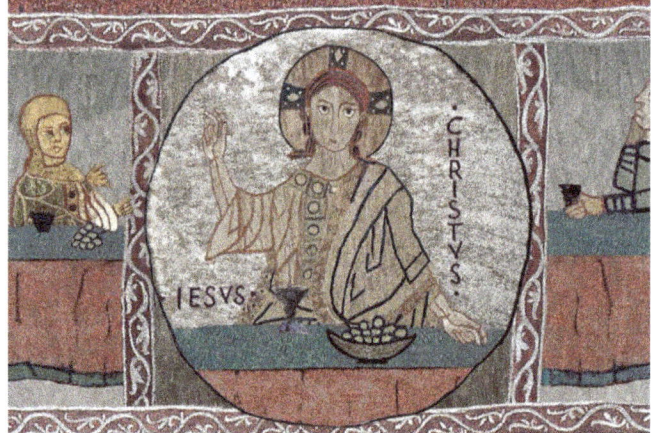

deemer, He fits in to the outer frame of the Tapestry with its illustrations of everyday life. Being of central importance to the religious content of the Creation Tapestry, His depiction represents a seamless continuation

---

[226] Cf. Palol, "Une broderie catalane," 191, ill. 10.

on from the Legend of the Holy Cross. Furthermore, it would be almost inconceivable for a medieval pictorial representation of the magnitude of the Creation Tapestry with its comprehensive religious content to be without an image of the Messiah, as God Incarnate in this world.[227]

There remains the question of the six remaining panels, three to the left and three to the right of the Christ figure. My suggestion is the twelve disciples, two in each panel. Thus, the religious message of the Tapestry would be meaningfully completed and the strictly symmetrical right/left concept of the Tapestry would have been taken into account. Moreover, the program of illustrations would be rounded off by such a reference to the New Testament. In the scene of the Last Supper, once again our attention is called to the deep connection between the everyday world of the here and now and the immaterial world of God beyond time. My suggestion for solving the problem of these six panels does not contradict other Romanesque pictorial sequences. A sequence of pictures on the apocalypse done in the Romanesque way would also be conceivable, though this would be much more difficult to fit into the strict symmetry of the Creation Tapestry.[228]

If my suggestion for the reconstruction of the Tapestry were valid in its essential elements (there is a certain probability that this is the case), we could ask ourselves about the meaning of this particular fragmentation of the Tapestry for our time. What meaning does it have for us that the central motif symbolizing the painful realization of the opposites went missing, that the images depicting the anguished tension of being caught between cosmic forces and the forces of chaos, between culture and nature went missing, that the Cross as a symbol of the union of the opposites but also as a symbol of the suffering which needs to be endured to achieve wholeness in mankind went missing, that all these cardinal elements as part of the macro- and microcosmic mandala of the Tapestry went missing? Without these pieces, the harmony of the mandala as a whole is disturbed. The central feminine principle of the Tapestry recedes into the background and the light/dark, male/female God becomes a purely masculine, "loving" God.

Seen from this angle, the reconstruction of the missing parts of the Tapestry is a burning necessity for us today for it is precisely from this one-sided image of God that we suffer. Our survival depends upon whether

---

[227] At that time, the cross and Christ were often used synonymously.
[228] See fn. 32.

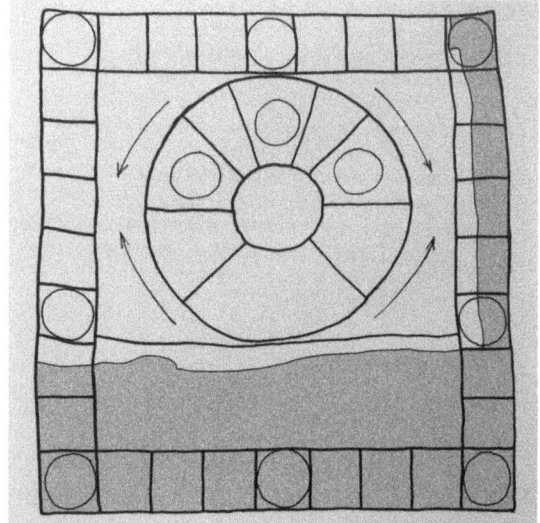

or not we are able to integrate the feminine and dark aspects of God shown to us in the Creation Tapestry, including those aspects of the divine which are bound to nature, all of which are absent in our present image of God, before time runs out and before our "strictly masculine do-good" attitude unwittingly destroys the foundations of our life.

The Creation Tapestry – A Catalonian Canopy

When, in 874, Duke Guifre El Pilos (William the Hairy) of Barcelona finally managed to free his dukedom from the Frankish crown, Catalonia became an important center of medieval culture, and on top of it, it was the only sovereign Christian territory on the Spanish coast of the Mediterranean for the next 300 years. Legend has it that the Catalan coat of arms was created when Charles the Bald drew four of his fingers which were wet with blood from a wound near the heart of the Duke of Barcelona, across his as yet undecorated golden shield.

In 1002, after the death of the victorious Moorish governor, Almansur, who had destroyed Barcelona in 987 and Santiago de Compostela ten years later, the realm of the Omanides disintegrated rapidly into several Taijas (partial principalities) and the Reconquista went ahead at full force. In 1054, at the time of the schism between Rome and Byzantium, Duke Ramon Berenguer I of Barcelona decreed the Catalan code of feudal law. It was around this time, that is, at the advent of Catalan's history of independence, that pilgrimages through the Pyrenees to the tomb of the apostle James the Elder in Santiago de Compostela became increasingly important for the Roman Catholic Church. Indeed, Catalonia's golden age had begun.

From the 12th century onward, it was the people of this bold, proud but peaceful nation who determined all aspects of life, including the political as well as intellectual and artistic realms, for tolerance, freedom, and democracy ruled and crass differences were less likely to occur here than elsewhere. Equality, freedom from prejudice, enlightenment, and even the emancipation of women became a matter of course from the 12th century onward. Heroes were neither soldiers nor knights, but rather free and independent merchants and proud farmers. Here was the fertile earth in which the art of the minstrels could grow. Even kings wrote poetry and shared their poetical love-songs with their court. Catalonia became the country of knights, troubadours and free spirits who were devoted to the "Gaya Scienza," the "joyful science," in which spirituality, reality, and mysticism were given equal measure.

According to Rudloff, this ability to make a bridge between things is a part of Catalan's originality. It demonstrates their ability to integrate opposites and to live courageously and constructively with painful contradictions.[229] This characteristic is given pictorial expression in mandalas which represent the archetype of wholeness. We also come across it in legendary form in the saga of the argonauts. Under the leadership of Jason, the argonauts disembarked at Port Vendres in Rousillou, near Cape Corbere, in search of the mysterious Golden Fleece. In the Middle Ages, their search became the pilgrimage to Santiago de Compostela, to the tomb of the apostle James, the Elder, which had been discovered around 800 A.D., and who, up to the present time, is still venerated as the patron saint of Spain (25th July).

The other important place of pilgrimage from the Spanish Middle Ages is on Monserrat. That there was a connection between this holy mountain of Catalonia, which legend says was cut out of the pinkish-grey limestone by angels and demons with golden saws, and the legend of the Holy Grail was known by both Wilhelm von Humboldt and Johann Wolfgang von Goethe. In ancient times, the Black Madonna, affectionately called "Moreneta," is said to have been worshipped here in a temple dedicated to Venus and later by hermits of the early Christian era who found the statue in a cave. Even today, as "the Queen of Catalonia," people regard her with the utmost reverence and esteem. Symbolically, she is the spiritual center of Catalan culture.

Another legendary figure who is important in Catalan is the figure of Hercules. The Romans called the road connecting Italy to Spain "Hercules' Road" and Monaco was called "Portus Hercules." Apparently, in ancient times, his gravestone was to be found in the cave of Lambives in the Pyrenees. At Cap Corbere, this Greek

---

[229] Rudloff, *Romanisches Katalonien*, 24.

hero is said to have entered the Underworld which was guarded by the three-headed hell-dog, Cerberus, in order to lead Persephone, the daughter of Demeter, back into this world.[230]

Both the legends about the birth of Catalonia and the few historical facts mentioned above portray a picture of medieval Catalonia as being a place sustained by a masculine and a feminine spirituality,[231] which is mirrored in the "sardana," the national folk-dance of Catalonia. In this dance, the male and female dancers turn slowly in a circle in 6/8 time, following a set pattern of steps while holding each other on the shoulders and facing the center of the circle. Anybody can join in at any point, dance, and leave again at will. The dance is slow enough for both the very young and old to participate without any difficulty. The orchestra, the "cobla," consists of eleven musicians. Along with the guitar, there is a shawm (Schalmei), a tambourine, a horn, an oboe, a trombone, and a double-bass. There is even a description of the "sardana" by Homer, and it is thought to have been created by Sardus, a son of Hercules. This round-dance is a danced-mandala in which all opposites are unified and surmounted. It is a symbol of the unity of Catalan society and has essentially female qualities. When the dancers perform in national costume, the men wear "barettinas," the red-woollen berets of the peasants and fishermen, as a symbol of freedom, equality, and brotherhood, and it was this same red beret which, in France in the 18th century, was worn by the Jacobins to indicate their fraternity with the radical revolutionaries.

Along with tolerance, unity, solidarity based upon communal feeling, compassion and rounded-wholeness, the "sardana" also demonstrates independence, dynamic action, autonomy, freedom, and the ability to persevere. Thus, the "sardana" portrays a male/female mandala, which, as a danced-symbol of the Catalan archetype, is of undiminished vigor, even today.

The Arab community of the 13th and 14th century erected public baths within a stone's throw of the former monastery buildings of the Gerona cathedral in which the Creation Tapestry is on display today. The Caldarium exists in virtually perfect condition right up to the present day. It consists of a square room with stone benches for resting upon along the outside walls, with a decorative octagonal well under a dome in

---

[230] Ibid., 24ff.
[231] Rudloff has written an excellent account.

the center of the room. The floorplan of this room corresponds to a mandala. This is not surprising in view of the fact that throughout the entire northern hemisphere, a steam-bath, which induces sweating, is looked upon as being part of a ritual of inner and outer cleansing before any important ceremony. The close proximity of Arabic baths to the cathedral, and this at a time when Islam was in the final stages of withdrawal from Spain, indicates how the Christian and Islamic cultures were able to live vigorously side by side; how they were able to be close and yet remain distinct, connected and yet independent of each other, two huge cultural complexes co-existing within the boundary of *one* city wall. Such a circumstance presupposes not only tolerance and cooperation, but also independence and perseverance. Bearing in mind this archetypal background of Catalonia in the late Middle Ages, the making of the Creation Canopy has great meaning. Such an inner and outer constellation permitted one person to make an inspired design that captured an unconscious image of the Christian micro- and macrocosm as an answer to the challenge of Islam. Although it was designed according to the iconographical norms in use at that time, it has lost none of its power to move people, even today.

The Creation Tapestry of Gerona, created around 1100 A.D., as the fruit of the tension that existed between the three great cultures of the Western hemisphere (Judaism, Christianity, and Islam), was perhaps even woven within the walls of the monastery of the cathedral of Gerona, which had, at the time, a highly renowned scriptorium. Possibly the creation part of the Tapestry was used as a canopy, while the part depicting the Legend of the Holy Cross extended down the wall behind the altar as a wall-hanging in, perhaps, the Chapel of the Holy Cross, "El Sepulcre," near to the main entrance of the Romanesque cathedral.

Prior to 1362, an embossed silver canopy was made for the new Gothic main altar. Was this meant to replace the damaged Creation Canopy of the old Romanesque altar? The Gothic canopy does not have an image of the Pantocrator at its center, but rather that of the coronation of the Blessed Virgin Mary, that is, an image which expresses the collective recognition of the archetype of the feminine principle, and which precisely sums up the content of its predecessor.

Because the Creation Tapestry incorporates all the main features of a mandala, it is able to present the symbols of which the God-image of Christians in the Late Middle Ages was comprised in both an orderly and concise manner. This had an effect upon the viewer for it led him to the center, to the essence of his belief and thereby safeguarded him from foreign influences. These foreign influences came partly from the Muslims who, by means of their successful campaign right across Spain and into the middle of Europe, had undertaken to take over the new territories. They brought with them their own knowledge of classical antiquity, which they had both refined and developed further. Thus, their influence upon the culture of newly-awakened Europe was profound.

Simultaneously, the highly-differentiated mystical tradition of Islam in the form of Sufism as it was practiced in the late Middle Ages was blossoming and bearing fruit, among which are the numerous writings of Ibn 'Arabi, who, like other great Sufis before and after him, was born in Spain. For the Sufis, inner experience was at the center of their contemplation, that is, their ability to have an inner experience of God, of His all-embracing timeless and spaceless existence in all things and in His everlasting act of creation.

Judaism, too, was blossoming in Spain of the late Middle Ages, a blossoming which culminated in the creation of the Kabbala.

At the time of Romanesque Spain when all three great cultural groups were accommodating toward each other, yet simultaneously remained distinct, when they were, above all, interwoven and having a fertilizing effect upon each other, there existed a consciousness in which everything, from the smallest thing to the largest, from the most insignificant thing to the most eminent, was given a meaningful place within the scheme of things. Inner and outer experience were closely connected and the one had an effect upon the other. The micro- and macrocosm mirrored each other. The separation of ego and world, of inner and outer, of psyche and matter which dominate our new-age consciousness had not yet taken place. The Romanesque view of life is sacramental, with its apocalyptic consciousness spanning the Great Divide between life and death, heaven and hell. Images are always comprised of *both an inner and an outer vision* and they are rooted directly in the archaic, magical layers of the unconscious. While they serve to portray nature's exterior face, nevertheless they are, above all, an expression of an inner, or spiritual, reality. The Romanesque common man of the late Middle Ages still had a connection to the eternal stream of images flowing out of his soul, and his art and architecture were an expression of his attempt to make his psychic truths visible.[232]

---

[232] "For this reason, every Romanesque image appears to be symbolic for it is based upon inner experience and not nature viewed on the

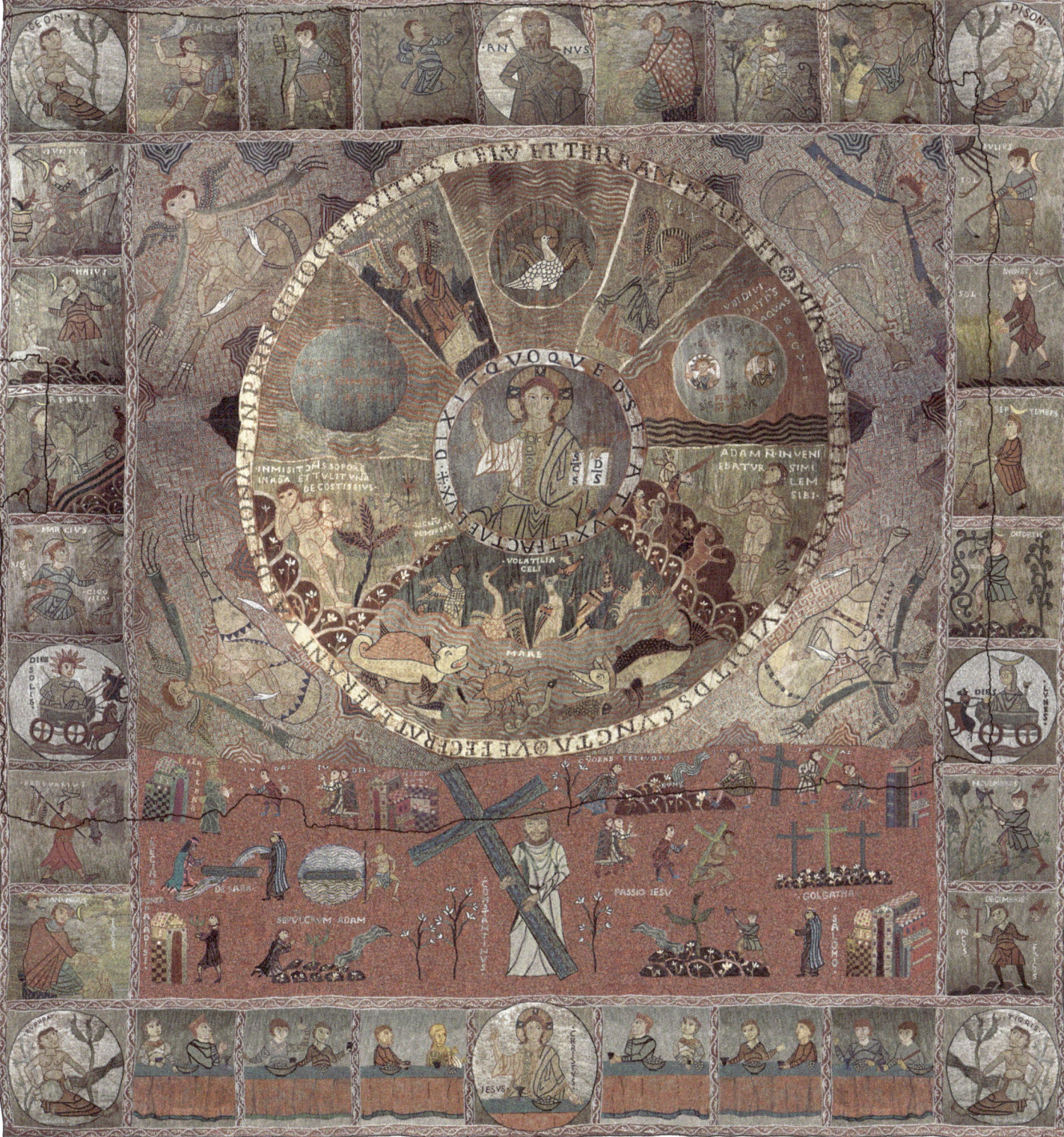

Today, many people are trying to overcome the meaningless naturalism and one-sided rational materialism of our time, barren as it is of images, by re-establishing a connection to the immortal truths that come to us in symbolic form in archetypal images. Thus, today there is a new appreciation of Romanesque art and its culture, as can be seen by the abundant textbooks, picture books, guide books on art, and so on, as well as by the many visitors to Catalonia. The Creation Tapestry in the museum of the cathedral of Gerona is one of the attractions. Even though it is not well-known, it attracts many thousands of visitors each year, most of whom linger in front of it, for they feel moved in some inexplicable and mysterious way.

Set within a framework of measured time, of months, seasons and years, the Creation Tapestry shows everyday life of the late Middle Ages with its recurrent outdoor work. The constant and unrelieved emergence of life in the here and now, as well as its passing, is only the outer framework of reality as we experience it, a reality that only becomes meaningful in the light of a greater reality upon which it is based. The reality we perceive with our senses does indeed extend itself to the edges of the world, where unconquerable mountains loom. But behind this world the Divine Spirit reigns, which can transform all potential creation into concrete reality. This leads inexorably to the center of cosmic existence. This is our connection to the cosmic center of all existence to which all life flows, and out of which all life comes.[233]

The center of the Creation Tapestry represents the all-encompassing world of the beyond which is invisible to man, although his whole existence is rooted there. Representing this supernatural world at the center is an image which depicts the primordial beginning of a masculine/feminine totality of all creation, a totality which has always been present with its dark/light double-nature since the first day of creation. Out of this center come the primary preconditions for life, that is, space, matter, and time, which emerged on the second, third, and fourth days of Creation. This foundation makes it possible for the "Quinta Essentia," the emanation of life, that is, plants, fish, birds and mammals, as well as Adam and Eve, to unfold. In this way, the Creation Story points, on the one hand, to an *a priori* already existent, meaningful principle of order. On the other hand, it suggests a causal principle of cause and effect to be at work, in that in the Christian creation myth,

---

[233] "When observing Romanesque imagery, the path leads one from the finite and temporal to the infinite and immortal, from the visible to the invisible." Ibid., 24. "It is not concerned with what is physically tangible and visible, but rather with what can be inwardly experienced." Ibid., 26. (Translated by Kappes)

it is assumed that development takes place from the simple to the complex, and from the general to the specific.

Thus, the entire Creation Tapestry represents an inspired attempt to portray the Romanesque God-image and to describe its inner connection. In the process, the artist unconsciously created a male/female God-image, combining both the inner, spiritual reality with outer reality.

As well as being an image of the whole cosmos and the Christian God, the Creation Tapestry is equally an image of the whole man, the Anthropos, who is comprised of consciousness as well as the boundless unconscious. The spirit, the dynamic aspect of the unconscious, permits the potential, which it has had within itself from the beginning of time, to become concrete in each individual. Being connected to its own center, to its male/female Self, which also encompasses the whole personality, the spirit is lived out in the tension that exists between chaos and cosmos, continuously searching for the path to individuation, which lends meaning to life, and which, in the Creation Tapestry, is represented in the images for the months of the year. Both in the legend of the Holy Cross, as well as in the myth of the birth, death, and resurrection of Jesus, the pictorial content of the Creation Tapestry puts great emphasis upon the painful tension man experiences between spirit and matter, between father and mother, but also between cosmos and chaos, between heaven and hell. By dying on the cross, Christ triumphed over death for the Christians, for the sacrifice of His life allowed each individual to share in the transcendental totality of His act. It is only through suffering that life achieves its true meaning.

By means of the vision it embodies and its translation into images, the Creation Tapestry anticipates what has since been made known in the field of modern natural science, and what has become the object of study in the area of depth psychology according to C. G. Jung. Concrete life takes place within space and time, within the confines of matter and psyche and it manifests itself both in a retrospectively causal manner as well as in a final, synchronistic way. The creation and development of each individual is bound up with archetypal events, behind which stands a transcendental connection to a unified world that is beyond our perception, the *unus mundus*.

In this way, acts of creation arise out of time immemorial and are brought into the here and now. The primordial, impassionate divine order *is* unbalanced. Only because this is so can concrete life happen. And it happens within the tension of chaos and cosmos, of destruction and release, on the one hand, and construction and achieving wholeness on the other. Creation out of the void is continuously taking place, together with annihilation and death which are also omnipresent. But there is yet another way in which the Creation Tapestry's images tie in with our modern world. Just as people in the 11th and 12th centuries were, today, we too are confronted with an increasingly apocalyptic view of the future, mainly because of the enormous potential of destructive power of the superpowers, along with the accelerated destruction of nature under the debris of our culture. Now, as then, there is a tendency coming from the unconscious to integrate the dark, feminine principle into the world of the light, masculine Logos.

We can recognize this tendency in its extroverted form among individual highly-motivated women, or groups of women and other emancipatory movements. In its introverted form, it represents a challenge for women to strongly adhere to their feminine nature. Simultaneously, men face the difficult task of perceiving and then taking seriously their own feminine aspect, the anima, which is a part of their soul. Only by means of these inner changes taking place will it be possible to change our patriarchal image of God into a feminine/masculine totality. The "Declaratio Assumptionis Mariae" made by Pope Pius XII at the Council of 1950 is a recognition of this necessity, as is the drawing power of the places of pilgrimage of the Black Madonna. Tying in with this is the fact that there has been a remarkable increase in the number of visions people throughout the world have had of the Virgin Mary.

It was C. G. Jung's conviction that the integration of the feminine in general is a task required of us all. In many of his writings, he repeatedly asks us to get our aggression under control if we wish to avoid the danger of a global catastrophe, which our purely masculine behavior toward nature and matter has evoked. "But reason has always proven too weak to cope with such a deep primordial urge. A greater power is needed to match the one-sidedness of purely aggressive behavior. That other power is the constellation of an opposing archetype, which today is the archetype of the feminine and which so far never has been integrated into our

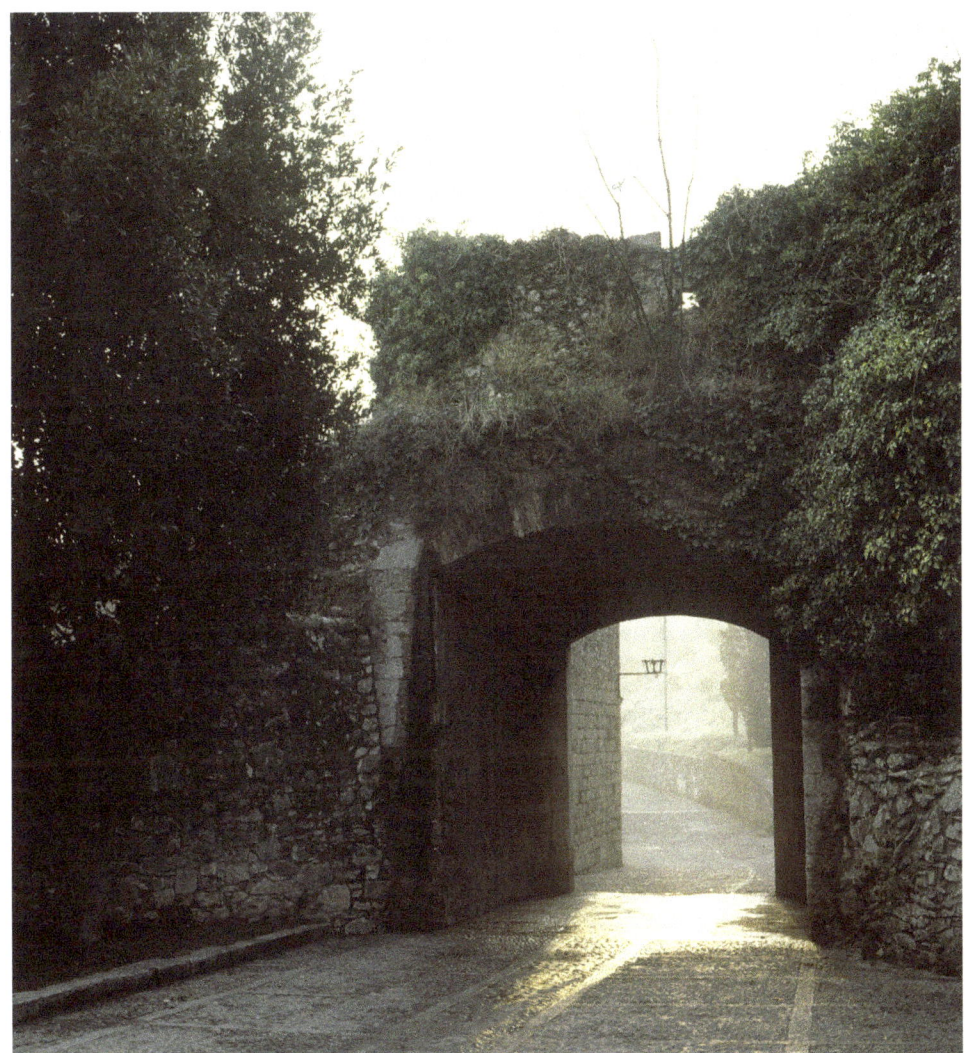

religious and scientific images of the world."[234]

Thus, the pictorial messages of the Creation Tapestry of Gerona are not simply historical reminiscences. Rather, the Tapestry's images present us with a challenge which is both relevant and crucial for the future, for it is capable of having a great healing effect upon us all.

---

[234] Von Franz, *C. G. Jung*, 146. On this, see also Isler, who in his paper on the Song of Margaret writes: "In a culture that has no feminine God, women cannot truly thrive. This is the essence of their distress. Indeed, taken to the extreme, all of nature cannot thrive: the trees, the waters, the air. We are slowly beginning to realize this." Isler, "Das Margaretenlied," 18. (Translated by Kappes)

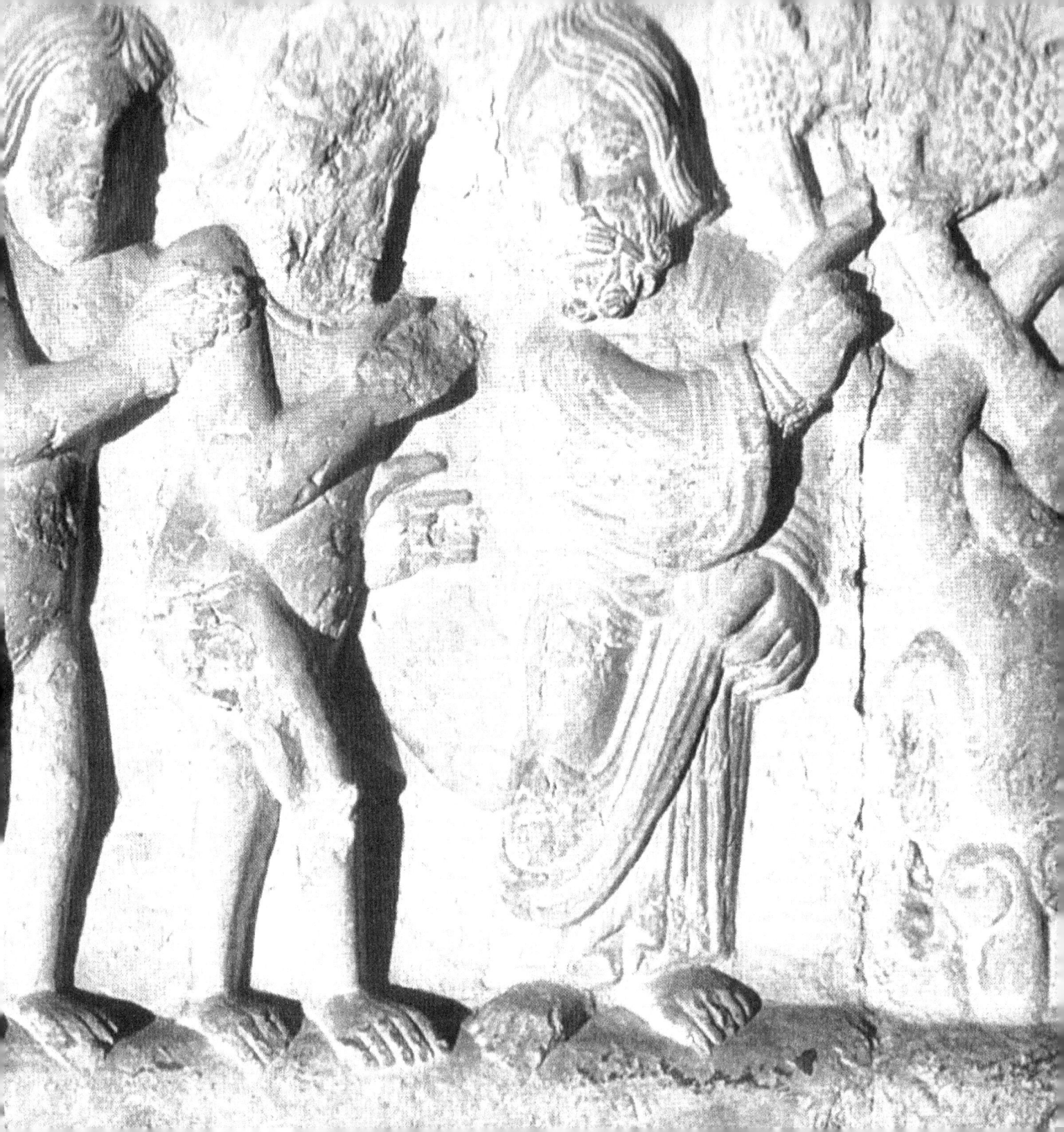

Bibliography

Augustinus, Aurelius. *Aufstieg zu Gott*. Zeugnisse mystischer Welterfahrung. Edited and translated with an introduction by Ladislaus Boros. Olten: Walter-Verlag, 1982.

Bakhtiar, Laleh. *Sufi: Expressions of the Mystic Quest*. London: Thames and Hudson, 1976.

Bash, K. W., Mario Jacobi, Marie-Louise von Franz, H. K. Fierz, Adolf Guggenbühl-Craig, and Walter Uhsadel. *Der unwahrscheinliche Jung: Beiträge zum 100. Geburtstag von C. G. Jung*. Zurich: Classen, 1977.

Battle I Prats, Luis. "El brodat de la Creació i el brodat de la invenció de la Santa Creu." *Revista de Girona* 92 (1980): 211–15.

Calzada, Josep. "El mosaic de la sinagoga de Beth-Alpha i el Tapís de la Creació de la Catedral de Girona." *Revista de Girona* 92 (1980): 173–205.

Camprodon, Jaume. "Pòrtic." *Revista de Girona* 92 (1980): 149.

Champeaux, de Gérard, and Dom Sébastian Sterckx. *Introduction au monde des Symboles*. Paris: Zodiaque, 1966.

Cumont, Franz. *Die Mysterien des Mithra: Ein Beitrag zur Religionsgeschichte der römischen Kaiserzeit*. Leipzig: Teubner, 1911.

Etter, Hansueli F. "Der Einsiedler Meinrad vom Finstern Wald." In *Jungiana: Beiträge zur Psychologie von C. G. Jung*, Reihe A, Band 1, 51–94. Küsnacht: Verlag Stiftung für Jung'sche Psychologie, 1989.

——. "Evolution und Tiefenpsychologie: Eine Synthese." *Archives suisses d'anthropologie générale* 46 (1982): 17–31.

——. "Psyche und Materie aus der Sicht der Jung'schen Psychologie." In *Grenzprobleme der Wissenschaften*, 27–37. Edited by Paul Feyerabend and Christian Thomas. Zurich: Verlag der Fachvereine, 1985.

——. *Sankt Meinrad*. Wendelinsverlag: Einsiedeln, 1984.

——. *Die Zürcher Stadtheiligen Felix und Regula: Legenden, Reliquien, Geschichte und ihre Botschaft im Licht moderner Forschung*. Zurich: Hochbauamt der Stadt Zürich/Büro für Archäologie, 1988.

Font Gratacós, Lamberto. "El Tapiz de la Creación de la Catedral de Gerona: Ensayos de estudio para una monografía." *Annals de l'Institut d'Estudis Gironins* 1 (1946): 160–71.

Girbal, Enrique C. "Tapiz notable de la Catedral de Gerona." *Revista de Girona* 92 (1980): 207–10. First publication in *Revista de Girona* 8 (1884): 1.8.

Goethe, Johann Wolfgang von. *Goethes Werke in zehn Bänden*. 10 Vols. Edited by Ernst Beutler.

    ——. *Dramen: Faust, eine Tragödie*. Vol. 4. Zurich, Artemis, 1961.

    ——. *Dramen: Früheste dramatische Fragmente und die Alexandriner Dramen*. Vol. 3. Zurich: Artemis, 1962.

    ——. *Poems and Epigrams*. Selected, translated and with an introduction by Michael Hamburger. London: Anvil Press Poetry, 1983.

González Mena, María Angeles. "Dos tapíces bordados medievales: El de la Creación en Gerona y el de Bayeux." *Revista de Girona* 92 (1980): 159–72.

Greene, Liz. *The Astrology of Fate*. Boston, MA: Weiser Books, 1984.

Grenfell, Bernard P., and Arthur S. Hunt. *New Sayings of Jesus and Fragment of a Lost Gospel*. Oxford: Horace Hart, 1904.

Gudiol i Cunill, Josep. *Els primitius: La pintura sobre fusta*. Vol. 2. Barcelona, 1929.

Hildegard of Bingen. *Hildegard von Bingen*. Zeugnisse mystischer Welterfahrung. Edited with an introduction by Heinrich Schipperges. Olten: Walter-Verlag, 1983.

——. *On Natural Philosophy and Medecine: Selections from Cause et Cure*. Translated from Latin with an introduction, notes and an interpretive essay by Margret Berger. Cambridge: D. S. Brewer, 1999.

——. *Welt und Mensch: "De operatione Dei" aus dem Gentner Kodex*. Translated with an introduction and notes by Heinrich Schipperges. Salzburg: Otto Müller Verlag, 1965.

———

Ibn al 'Arabi, Abu Bakr Muhammed. *The Wisdom of the Prophets*. Translated from Arabic to French with notes by Titus Burckhardt and from French to English by Angela Culme-Seymour. Aldsworth, GLS: Beshara Publications, 1975.

Isler, Gotthilf. "Das rätoromanische Margaretenlied – Eine seelische Tragödie." *Terraplana* 4 (1988): 10–18.

———. *Die Sennenpuppe: Eine Untersuchung über die religiöse Funktion einiger Alpensagen*. Basel: Schweizerische Gesellschaft für Volkskunde, 1971.

Jacobus de Voragine. *The Golden Legend*. Translated and adapted from the Latin by Granger Ryan and Helmut Ripperger. New York: Arno Press, 1969.

Jaffé, Aniela. *Aus C. G. Jungs Welt: Gedanken und Politik. Vier Aufsätze*. Zurich: Classen, 1979.

Jung, C. G. *Bollingen Series XX: The Collected Works of C. G. Jung*. 20 Vols. Edited by Herbert Read, Michael Fordham, Gerhard Adler, and William McGuire. Translated by R. F. C. Hull.

  ———. *Aion: Researches into the Phenomenology of the Self*. 2nd ed. Vol. 9/II. Princeton, NJ: Princeton University Press, 1978.

  ———. *Alchemical Studies*. Vol. 13. Princeton, NJ: Princeton University Press, 1983.

  ———. *The Archetypes and the Collective Unconscious*. 2nd ed. Vol. 9/I. Princeton, NJ: Princeton University Press, 1980.

  ———. *Mysterium Coniunctionis: An Inquiry into the Separation and Synthesis of Psychic Opposites in Alchemy*. 2nd ed. Vol. 14. Princeton, NJ: Princeton University Press, 1989.

  ———. *Psychology and Alchemy*. 2nd ed. Vol. 12. Princeton, NJ: Princeton University Press, 1993.

  ———. *Psychology and Religion: West and East*. 2nd ed. Vol. 11. Princeton, NJ: Princeton University Press, 1989.

  ———. *The Structure and Dynamics of the Psyche*. 2nd ed. Vol. 8. Princeton, NJ: Princeton University Press, 1981.

  ———. *Symbols of Transformation*. 2nd ed. Vol. 5. Princeton, NJ: Princeton University Press, 1990.

———. *Letters*. Vol. 2, 1951–1961. Selected and edited by Gerhard Adler, in collaboration with Aniela Jaffé. Translated by R. F. C. Hull. 2 Vols. London: Routledge & Kegan Paul, 1976.

Jung, C. G., Marie-Louise von Franz, Joseph L. Henderson, Jolande Jacobi, and Aniela Jaffé. *Man and his Symbols*. London: Aldus Books Limited, 1964.

Jung, Emma, and Marie-Louise von Franz. *The Grail Legend*. 2nd ed. Translated by Andrea Dykes. Boston, MA: Sigo Press, 1986.

Keckeis, Peter, ed. „D'Tifelsbrugg und d'r Tifelsstei." In *Sagen der Schweiz: Uri*, 31. Zurich: Ex Libris, 1985.

Kendrick, Albert F. "Textiles." In *Spanish Art: An Introductory Review of Architecture, Painting, Sculpture, Textiles, Ceramics, Woodwork, Metalwork*. Burlington Magazine Monographs, edited by Robert Rattray Tatlock, vol. 2, 59–70. London: B. T. Batsdorf Ltd., 1929.

Lammers, Ann Conrad, Adrian Cunningham, and Murray Stein, eds. *The Jung-White Letters*. London: Routledge, 2007.

Legner, Anton. *Monumenta Annonis: Köln und Siegburg. Weltbild und Kunst im hohen Mittelalter: Eine Dokumentation zur Ausstellung des Schnütgen-Museums der Stadt Köln*. Cologne, 1975.

Marqués Casanovas, Jaume. "El Tapíz de la Creació en el seu context." *Revista de Girona* 92 (1980): 217–24.

Martinell, Cèsar. "El tesoro artistico de Cataluniã: El Panõ de la Creación de Gerona." In *Barcelona Atracction* 208, 209 (1928): 305ff., 359ff.

Mundo, Anscari M. "L'escriptura del Tapíz de la Creació de la Catedral de Girona." *Revista de Girona* 92 (1980): 157–58.

Palol, Pedro de. "Une broderie catalane d'èpoque romane: La Genèse de Gérone." *Cahiers Archéologiques* 8 (1956): 175–251.

———. *El Tapíz de la Creació de la Catedral de Girona*. Barcelona: Edicions Proa, 1986.

Pijoan, Josep. *Summa Artis: Historia general del Arte*. Vol 7. Madrid: Espasa Calpe, 1948.

Quispel, Gilles. "Die Schwarze Madonna." Lecture, Psychological Club, Zurich, Mai 18, 1975.

Riedel, Ingrid. *Farben in Religion, Gesellschaft, Kunst und Psychotherapie*. Stuttgart: Kreuz-Verlag, 1983.

Riemann, Fritz. *Lebenshilfe Astrologie: Gedanken und Erfahrungen*. Munich: Klett-Cotta, 1976.

Ring, Thomas. *Astrologie ohne Aberglaube*. Düsseldorf: Econ, 1972.

Rudloff, Diether. *Romanisches Katalonien: Kunst, Kultur, Geschichte*. Stuttgart: Urachhaus, 1980.

———. *Zillis: Die romanische Bilderdecke der Kirche St. Martin*. Basel: Verlag Peter Herman, 1989.

Schimmel, Annemarie. *Mystical Dimensions of Islam*. Chapel Hill, NC: University of North Carolina Press, 1975.

——. *Die Träume des Kalifen: Träume und ihre Deutung in der islamischen Kultur*. Munich: C. H. Beck, 2000.

Scholem, Gershom. *Die Geheimnisse der Schöpfung: Ein Kapitel aus dem kabbalistischen Buch Sohar*. Frankfurt am Main: Insel Verlag, 1971.

Schrödinger, Erwin. "Our image of matter." In *On Modern Physics*, translated by M. Goodman and J. W. Binns, 37–56. London: The Orient Press Ltd, 1961.

Schwarzer Hirsch. *Die heilige Pfeife: Das indianische Weisheitsbuch der sieben geheimen Riten*. Recorded by Joseph Epes Brown, with an epilog by Frithjof Schuon. Bornheim: Lamuv, 1983.

Taberner i Collellmir, Josep M. "El Tapíz de la Creació de la Catedral de Girona." *Arte religioso actual*, 65–66, (no year), separate print of the cathedral museum.

Von Franz, Marie-Louise. *C. G. Jung: His Myth in Our Time*. Translated by William H. Kennedy. New York: G. P. Putnam's Sons, 1975.

——. *Creation Myths: Patterns of Creativity mirrored in Creation Myths*. Dallas: Spring Publications, 1972.

——. *Individuation in Fairy Tales*. Boston, MA: Shambhala, 1990.

——. *The Interpretation of Fairy Tales*. Boston, MA: Shambhala, 1996.

——. *Number and Time: Reflections Leading toward a Unification of Depth Psychology and Physics*. Edited by James Hillman. Translated by Andrea Dykes. Evanston, IL: Northwestern University Press, 1974.

——. *On Divination and Synchronicity: The Psychology of Meaningful Chance*. Edited by Daryl Sharp. Toronto: Inner City Books, 1980.

——. *The Passion of Perpetua: A Psychological Interpretation of Her Visions*. Edited by Daryl Sharp. Translated by Elisabeth Welsh. Toronto: University of Toronto Press, 2004.

——. *Projection and Re-Collection in Jungian Psychology: Reflections of the Soul*. Translated by William H. Kennedy. La Salle, IL: Open Court, 1980.

——. *Psyche and Matter*. Boston, MA: Shambhala, 1992.

——. *Symbolism in Fairy Tales*. Book 1–3. In preparation.

Wille, Bruno. *Darwins Weltanschauung*. Heilbronn: Salzer, 1906.

www.ingramcontent.com/pod-product-compliance
Lightning Source LLC
Chambersburg PA
CBHW041920180526
45172CB00013B/1339